Minister Manual

Confession of Faith and Minister's Manual

Containing the Confession of Faith Adopted at Dortrecht in 1632

Minister Manual

Confession of Faith and Minister's Manual
Containing the Confession of Faith Adopted at Dortrecht in 1632

ISBN/EAN: 9783743342095

Manufactured in Europe, USA, Canada, Australia, Japa

Cover: Foto ©ninafisch / pixelio.de

Manufactured and distributed by brebook publishing software (www.brebook.com)

Minister Manual

Confession of Faith and Minister's Manual

CONFESSION OF FAITH

AND

MINISTERS MANUAL

CONTAINING

THE CONFESSION OF FAITH ADOPTED AT DORTRECHT IN 1632 — THE SHORTER CATECHISM—FORMS FOR BAPTISM, THE LORD'S SUPPER, MARRIAGE, ORDINATION OF BISHOPS AND MINISTERS — FUNERAL LESSONS, TEXTS, ETC.

Christ also loved the Church, and gave himself for it;
That he might sanctify and cleanse it with the washing of water by the word,
That he might present it to himself a glorious Church, not having spot or wrinkle, or any such thing; but that it should be holy and without blemish. Eph. 5. 25—27.

ELKHART, INDIANA.
MENNONITE PUBLISHING COMPANY.
1890.

Entered according to act of Congress in the year 1890,
By MENNONITE PUBLISHING CO., ELKHART, IND.,
In the Office of the Librarian of Congress at Washington.

PREFACE.

Many members, and especially ministers of the Mennonite Church have long felt the need of a book, in the English language, containing, in compact form, our confession of faith, as well as the forms for the different church services. In this little volume it is our purpose to supply this want.

The Confession of Faith is the same that has been in use among our people for over two hundred and fifty years. The forms for the different services were partly translated from the German work published in Canada, by Bish. Benjamin Eby, in 1840, and partly arranged from various manuscripts containing forms, now in use in the church, in different parts of the country.

Some of these differed widely in substance, form and language. It has been our aim to arrange a set of forms well adapted to the purpose for which they are intended, expressed in language easily understood, and in harmony with the present usages.

We believe that these forms, published and placed into the hands of the church, will be a great help to the minister in his work, and to the members in general. We feel sure that this little book will be both a benefit and a satisfaction to young people and others who contemplate uniting with the church. It will also, no doubt, do much toward bringing about a closer union, and a greater uniformity between the churches in different localities. The outlay of money to obtain it will be so small that every member will be able to have one; and the book will be so small that it may be conveniently carried in the pocket. In this way our people may become better acquainted with both the forms of service, and the doctrines of our faith, which are matters of much importance in establishing and confirming the people in the teachings of the Bible and the church.

May God bless this little work as a means of awakening a warmer zeal for God and the church, and of uniting us all more closely in the love of Jesus.

THE PUBLISHERS.

Mennonite Confession of Faith

Written and adopted at a Peace Convention held at Dortrecht, on the 21st day of April, 1632,

ENTITLED:

A DECLARATION OF THE CHIEF ARTICLES OF OUR GENERAL CHRISTIAN FAITH.

ARTICLE I.

CONCERNING GOD AND THE CREATION OF ALL THINGS.

Whereas it is declared, that "without faith it is impossible to please God" (Heb. 11:6), and that "he that cometh to God must believe that he is, and that he is a rewarder of them that diligently seek him," therefore we confess with the mouth, and believe with the heart, together with all the pious, according to the Holy Scriptures, that there is one eternal, almighty, and incomprehensible God, Father, Son, and Holy Ghost, and none more and none other, before whom no God existed, neither will exist after him. For from him, through him, and in him are all things. To him be blessing, praise, and honor, for ever and ever. Gen. 17:1; Deut. 6:4; Isaiah 46:9; 1 John 5:7.

In this one God, who "worketh all in all," we believe. Him we confess as the Creator of all things, visible and invisible; who in six days created and prepared "heaven and earth, and the sea, and all things that are therein." And we further believe, that this God still governs and preserves the same, together with all his works, through his wisdom, his might, and the "word of his power". Gen. 5:1, 2; Acts. 14:15; 1 Cor. 12:6; Heb. 1:3.

When he had finished his works and, according to his good pleasure, had ordained and prepared each of them, so that they were right and good according to their nature, being and quality, he created the first man, Adam, the father of all of us, gave him a body formed "of the dust of the ground, and breathed into his nostrils the breath of life," so that he "became a living soul," created by God in his own image and likeness," in "righteousness and true holiness" unto eternal life. He also gave him a place above all other creatures and endowed him with many high and excellent gifts, put him into the garden of Eden, and gave him a commandment and an interdiction. Thereupon he took a rib from the said Adam, made a woman out of it, brought her to him, and gave her to him as a helpmate and housewife. Consequently he has caused, that from this first man, Adam, all men who "dwell on the face of the earth," have been begotten and have descended. Gen. 1:27; 2:7, 15, 17, 22; 5:1; Acts 17:26.

Article II.

The Fall of Man.

We believe and confess, that, according to the purport of the Holy Scriptures, our first parents, Adam and Eve, did not long remain in the happy state in which they were created; but did, after being seduced by the deceit and "subtility" of the serpent, and envy of the devil, violate the high command of God, and became disobedient to their Creator; through which disobedience "sin entered into the world, and death by sin;" so that "death passed upon all men, for that all have sinned," and thereby incurred the wrath of God and condemnation. For which reason our first parents were, by God, driven out of Paradise, to cultivate the earth, to maintain themselves thereon in sorrow, and to "eat their bread in the sweat of their face," until they "returned to the ground, from which they were taken." And that they did, therefore, through this one sin, so far apostatize, depart, and estrange themselves from God, that they could neither help themselves, nor be helped by any of their descendants, nor by angels, nor by any other creature in heaven or on earth, nor be redeemed or reconciled to God; but would have had to be lost forever, had not God, who pitied his creatures, in mercy, interposed in their behalf, and made provision for their restoration. Gen. 3:6, 23; Rom. 5:12—19; Psalm 47:8, 9; Rev. 5:3; John 3:16.

ARTICLE III.

THE RESTORATION OF MAN THROUGH THE PROMISE OF THE COMING OF CHRIST.

Regarding the restoration of our first parents and their descendants, we believe and confess: That God, notwithstanding their fall, transgression and sin, and although they had no power to help themselves, he was nevertheless not willing that they should be cast off entirely, or be eternally lost; but again called them unto him, comforted them, and showed them that there were yet means with him for their reconciliation; namely, the immaculate Lamb, the

Son of God; who "was fore-ordained" to this purpose "before the foundation of the world," and who was promised to them and all their descendants, while they (our first parents) were yet in paradise, for their comfort, redemption, and salvation; yea, who was given to them thenceforward, through faith, as their own; after which all the pious patriarchs, to whom this promise was often renewed, longed and searched, beholding it through faith at a distance, and expecting its fulfillment—expecting that he (the Son of God), would, at his coming, again redeem and deliver the fallen race of man from their sins, their guilt, and unrighteousness. John 1:29; 11:27; 1 Pet. 1:19; Gen. 3:15; 1 John 2:1, 2; 3:8; Gal. 4:4, 5.

Article IV.

The Advent of Christ into this World, and the Reason of His Coming.

We believe and confess further: That "when the fullness of the time was come," after which all the pious patriarchs so ardently longed, and which they so anxiously awaited—the previously promised Messiah, Redeemer, and Savior, proceeded from God, being sent by him, and, according to the prediction of the prophets and the testimony of the evangelists, came into the world, yea, into the flesh, so that the word itself thus became flesh and man; and that he was conceived by the Virgin Mary (who was espoused to a man named Joseph, of the house of David), and that she bare him as her firstborn son at Bethlehem, "wrapped him in swaddling clothes, and laid him in a manger." John 4:25; 16:28; 1 Tim. 3:16; Matt. 1:21; John 1:14; Luke 2:7.

Further we believe and confess, that this is the same One, "whose goings forth have been from of old, from everlasting;" who has "neither beginning of days, nor end of life." Of whom it is testified, that he is "Alpha and Omega, the beginning and the end, the first and the last." That this is also he—and none other—who was chosen, promised, and sent; who came into the world; and who is God's only, first, and proper Son; who was before John the Baptist, before Abraham, before the world; yea, who was David's Lord, and who is God of the "whole earth", "the first-born of every creature"; who was sent into the world, and himself delivered up the body prepared for him, as "an offering and a sacrifice to God for a sweet smelling savor;" yea, for the comfort, redemption, and salvation of all—of the human race. Micah 5:2; Heb. 7:3; Rev. 1:8; John 3:16; Rom. 8:32; Col. 1:15; Heb. 10:5.

But how, or in what manner, this worthy body was prepared, or how the word became flesh, and he himself man, we content ourselves with the declaration which the worthy evangelists have given and left in their description thereof; according to which we confess with all the saints, that he is the Son of the living God, in whom exist all our hope, comfort, redemption, and salvation, and which we are to seek in no one else. Luke 1:31—35; John 20:31.

Further, we believe and confess by authority of scripture, that when he had ended his course, and "finished" the work for which he was sent into the world, he was, by the providence of God, delivered into the hands of the unrighteous; suffered under the judge, Pontius Pilate, was crucified, died, was buried, rose again from the dead on the third day, and ascended into heaven, where he now sits at the right hand of the Majesty of God on high;" from whence he will come again to judge the living and the dead. Luke 23:1; 33:53; 24:5, 6, 51.

Thus we believe the Son of God died—"tasted death for every man," shed his precious blood, and thereby bruised the head of the serpent, destroyed the works of the devil, "blotted out the hand-writing," and purchased redemption for the whole human race; and thus he became the source of eternal salvation to all who from the time of Adam to the end of the world, shall have believed in him, and obeyed him. Gen. 3:15; 1 John 3:8; Col. 2:14; Rom. 5:18.

ARTICLE V.

THE LAW OF CHRIST, WHICH IS THE HOLY GOSPEL, OR THE NEW TESTAMENT.

We also believe and confess, that Christ before his ascension, established and instituted his New Testament and left it to his followers, to be and remain an everlasting testament, which he confirmed and sealed with his own precious blood; and in which he has so highly commended to them, that neither men nor angels may change it, neither take therefrom nor add thereto. Jer. 31:31; Heb. 9:15—17;

Matt. 26:28; Gal. 1:8; 1 Tim. 6:3; Rev. 22:18, 19; Matt. 5:18; Luke 21:33.

And that he has caused this testament (in which the whole counsel and will of his heavenly Father, so far as these are necessary to the salvation of man, are comprehended), to be proclaimed, in his name, through his beloved apostles, messengers, and servants (whom he chose and sent into all the world for this purpose)—to all nations, people and tongues; these apostles preaching repentance and remission of sins; and that he, in said testament, caused it to be declared, that all men without distinction, if they are obedient, through faith, follow, fulfill and live according to the precepts of the same, are his children and rightful heirs; having thus excluded none from the precious inheritance of eternal salvation, except the unbelieving and disobedient, the headstrong and unconverted; who despise such salvation; and thus by their own actions incur guilt by refusing the same, and "judge themselves unworthy of everlasting life." Mark 16:15; Luke 24:46, 47; Rom. 8:17; Acts 13:46.

Article VI.

Repentance and Amendment of Life.

We believe and confess, that, as the "imagination of man's heart is evil from his youth," and consequently inclined to all unrighteousness, sin and wickedness, that, therefore, the first doctrine of the precious New Testament of the Son of God is, Repentance and amendment of life. Gen. 8:21; Mark 1:15. Therefore those who have ears to hear, and hearts to understand, must "bring forth fruits meet for repentance," amend their lives, believe the gospel, "depart from evil and do good," desist from wrong and cease from sinning, "put off the old man with his deeds, and put on the new man," which after God is created in righteousness and true holiness." For neither *Baptism Sacrament,* nor *church-fellowship,* nor any other external ceremony, can, without faith, the new birth, and a change or renewal of life, help, or qualify us, that we may please God, or receive any consolation or promise of salvation from him. Luke 3:8; Eph. 4:22, 24; Col. 3:9, 10. But on the contrary, we must go to God "with a sincere heart in full assurance of faith," and believe in Jesus Christ, as the scriptures speak and testify of him. Through which faith we obtain the pardon of our sins, become sanctified, justified, and children of God; yea, partakers of his mind, nature and image, as we are born again of God through his incorruptible seed from above. Heb. 10:21, 22; John 7:38; 2 Pet. 1:4.

Article VII.—Holy Baptism.

Regarding baptism, we confess that all penitent believers, who through faith, the new birth and renewal of the Holy Ghost, have become united with God, and whose names are recorded in heaven, must, on such scriptural confession of their faith, and renewal of life, according to the command and doctrine of Christ, and the example and custom of the apostles, be baptized with water in the ever adorable name of the Father, and of the Son, and of the Holy Ghost, to the burying of their sins, and thus to become incorporated into the communion of the saints; whereupon they must learn to observe all things whatever the Son of God taught, left on record, and commanded his followers to do. Matt. 3:15; 28:19, 20; Mark 16:15, 16; Acts 2:38; 8:12, 38; 9:19; 10:47; 16:33; Rom. 6:3, 4; Col. 2:12.

Article VIII.
The Church of Christ.

We believe in and confess a visible Church of God, consisting of those, who, as before remarked, have truly repented, and rightly believed; who are rightly baptized, united with God in heaven, and incorporated into the communion of the saints on earth. 1 Cor. 12, 13. And these, we confess, are a "chosen generation, a royal priesthood, an holy nation," who have the testimony, that they are the "bride" of Christ; yea, that they are children and heirs of eternal life—a "habitation of God through the Spirit," built on the foundation of the apostles and prophets, of which "Christ himself is the chief corner stone"—the foundation on which his church is built. John 3:29; Matt. 16:18; Eph. 2:19—21; Tit. 3:7; 1 Pet. 1:18, 19; 2:9. This church of the living God, which he has purchased and redeemed through his own precious blood, and with which he will be—according to his own promise—for her comfort and protection, "always, even unto the end of the world;" yea, will dwell and walk with her and preserve her, that no "winds" nor "floods," yea, not even the "gates of hell shall prevail against her"—may be known by her evangelical faith, doctrine, love, and godly conversation; also by her pure walk and practice, and her observance of the true ordinances of Christ, which he has strictly enjoined on his followers. M 7:25, 18:18, 28:20; 2 Cor. 6:16.

ARTICLE IX.

THE OFFICE OF TEACHERS AND MINISTERS—MALE AND FEMALE—IN THE CHURCH.

Regarding the offices, and election of persons to the same, in the church, we believe and confess: That, as the church cannot exist and prosper, nor continue in its structure, without offices and regulations, that therefore the Lord Jesus has himself (as a father in his house), appointed and prescribed his offices and ordinances, and has given commandments concerning the same, as to how each one should walk therein, give heed to his own work and calling, and do it as it becomes him to do. Eph. 4:11, 12. For he himself, as the faithful and great Shepherd, and Bishop of our souls, was sent into the world, not to wound, to break, or destroy the souls of men, but to heal them; to seek that which is lost, and to pull down the hedges and partition wall, so as to make out of *many one*; thus collecting out of Jews and heathen, yea, out of all nations, a church in his name; for which (so that no one might go astray or be lost) he laid down his own life, and thus procured for them salvation, made them free and redeemed them, to which blessing no one could help them, or be of service in obtaining it. 1 Pet. 2:25; Matt. 18:11; Eph. 2:13, 14; John 10:9, 11, 15.

And that he, besides this, left his church before his departure, provided with faithful ministers, apostles, evangelists, pastors, and teachers, whom he had chosen by prayer and supplication through the Holy Spirit, so that they might govern the church, feed his flock, watch over, maintain, and care for the same; yea, do in all things as he left them an example, taught them, and commanded them to do; and likewise to teach the church to observe all things whatsoever he commanded them. Eph. 4:11; Luke 6:12, 13; 10:1; Matt. 28:20.

Also that the apostles were afterwards, as faithful followers of Christ and leaders of the church, diligent in these matters, namely, in choosing through prayer and supplication to

God, brethren who were to provide all the churches in the cities and circuits, with bishops, pastors, and leaders, and to ordain to these offices such men as took "heed unto themselves and unto the doctrine," and also unto the flock; who were sound in the faith, pious in their life and conversation, and who had—as well within the church as "without"—a good reputation and a good report; so that they might be a light and example in all godliness and good works; might worthily administer the Lord's ordinances— baptism and sacrament—and that they (the brethren sent by the apostles) might also, at all places, where such were to be had, appoint faithful men as elders, who were able to teach others, confirm them in the name of the Lord "with the laying on of hands," and who (the elders) were to take care of all things of which the church stood in need; so that they, as faithful servants, might well "occupy" their Lord's money, gain thereby, and thus "save themselves and those who hear them." 1 Tim. 3:1; 4:14— 16; Acts 1:23, 24; Tit. 1:5; Luke 19:13.

That they should also take good care (particularly each one of the charge over which he had the oversight), that all the circuits should be well provided with almoners, who should have the care and oversight of the poor, and who were to receive gifts and alms, and again faithfully to distribute them amongst the poor saints who were in need, and this in all honesty, as is becoming. Acts 6:3—6.

Also that honorable old widows should be chosen as servants, who, besides the almoners, are to visit, comfort, and take care of the poor, the weak, the afflicted, and the needy, as also to visit, comfort, and take care of widows and orphans; and further to assist in taking care of any matters in the church that properly come within their sphere, according to their best ability. 1 Tim. 5:9, 10; Rom. 16:1, 2.

And as it further regards the almoners, that they (particularly if they are fit persons, and chosen and ordained thereto by the church), may also in aid and relief of the bishops, exhort the church (being, as already remarked, chosen thereto), and thus assist in word and doctrine; so that each one may serve the other from love, with the gift which he has received from the Lord; so that through the common service and assistance of each member, according to his ability, the body of Christ may be edified, and the Lord's vineyard and church be preserved in its growth and structure. 2 Tim. 2:2.

Article X.
The Lord's Supper.

We also believe in and observe the breaking of bread, or the Lord's Supper, as the Lord Jesus instituted the same (with bread and wine) before his sufferings, and also observed and ate it with the apostles, and also commanded it to be observed to his remembrance, as also the apostles subseqently taught and observed the same in the church, and commanded it to be observed by believers in commemoration of the death and sufferings of the Lord—the breaking of his worthy body and the shedding of his precious blood—for the whole human race. So is the observance of this sacrament also to remind us of the benefit of the said death and sufferings of Christ, namely, the redemption and eternal salvation which he purchased thereby, and the great love thus shown to sinful man; whereby we are earnestly exhorted also to love one another—to love our neighbor—to forgive and absolve him—even as Christ has done unto us— and also to endeavor to maintain and keep alive the union and communion which we have with God, and amongst one another; which is thus shown and represented to us by the aforesaid breaking of bread. Matt. 26:26; Mark 14:22; Luke 22:19; Acts 2:42, 46; 1 Cor. 10:16; 11:23—26.

Article XI.

The Washing of the Saint's Feet.

We also confess a washing of the feet, of the saints, as the Lord Jesus did not only institute and command the same, but did also himself wash the feet of the apostles, although he was their Lord and master; thereby giving an example that they also should wash one another's feet, and thus do to one another as he did to them; which they also afterwards taught believers to observe, and all this as a sign of true humiliation; but yet more particularly as a sign to remind us of the true washing—the washing and purification of the soul in the blood of Christ. John 13:4—17; 1 Tim. 5:10.

Article XII.

Matrimony.

We also confess that there is in the church of God an "honorable" state of matrimony between two believers of the different sexes, as God first instituted the same in paradise between Adam and Eve, and as the Lord Jesus reformed it by removing all abuses which had crept into it, and restoring it to its first order. Gen. 1:27; 2:18, 22, 24.

In this manner the apostle Paul also taught and permitted matrimony in the church, leaving it to each one's own choice to enter into matrimony with any person who would unite with him in such state, provided that it was done "in the Lord," according to the primitive order; the words "in the Lord," to be understood, according to our opinion, that just as the patriarchs had to marry amongst their own kindred or generation, so there is also no other liberty allowed to believers under the New Testament Dispensation, than to marry amongst the "chosen generation," or the spiritual kindred of Christ; that is, to such—and none others—as are already, previous to their marriage, united to the church in heart and soul, have received the same baptism, belong to the same church, are of the same faith and doctrine, and lead the same course of life, with themselves. 1 Cor. 7; 9:5; Gen. 24:4; 28:6; Num. 36:6—9.

Such are then, as already remarked, united by God and the church according to the primitive order, and this is then called, "Marrying in the Lord." 1 Cor. 7:39.

Article XIII.
The Office of Civil Government.

We also believe and confess, that God has instituted civil government, for the punishment of the wicked and the protection of the pious; and also further, for the purpose of governing the world—governing countries and cities; and also to preserve its subjects in good order and under good regulations. Wherefore we are not permitted to despise, blaspheme, or resist the same; but are to acknowledge it as a minister of God and be subject and obedient to it, in all things that do not militate against the law, will, and commandments of God; yea, "to be ready to every good work;" also faithfully to pay it custom, tax, and tribute; thus giving it what is its due; as Jesus Christ taught, did himself, and commanded his followers to do. That we are also to pray to the Lord earnestly for the government and its welfare, and in behalf of our country, so that we may live under its protection, maintain ourselves, and "lead a quiet and peaceable life in all godliness and honesty." And further, that the Lord would recompense them (our rulers), here and in eternity, for all the benefits, liberties, and favors which we enjoy under their laudable administration. Rom. 13:1—7; Tit. 3:1, 2; 1 Pet. 2:17; Matt. 17:27; 22:21; 1 Tim. 2:1, 2.

Article XIV.
Defense by Force.

Regarding revenge, whereby we resist our enemies with the sword, we believe and confess, that the Lord Jesus has forbidden his disciples and followers all revenge and resistance, and has thereby commanded them not to "return evil for evil, nor railing for railing;" but to "put up the sword into the sheath," or, as the prophets foretold, "beat them into ploughshares." Matt. 5:39, 44; Rom. 12:14; 1 Pet. 3:9; Isaiah 2:4; Micah 4:3.

From this we see, that, according to the example, life, and doctrine of Christ, we are not to do wrong, or cause offense or vexation to any one; but to seek the welfare and salvation of all men; also, if necessity should require it, to flee, for the Lord's sake, from one city or country to another, and suffer the "spoiling of our goods," rather than give occasion of offense to any one; and if we are struck on our "right cheek, rather to turn the other also," than revenge ourselves, or return the blow. Matt. 5:39; 10:23; Rom. 12:19.

And that we are, besides this, also to pray for our enemies, comfort and feed them, when they are hungry or thirsty, and thus by well-doing convince them and overcome the evil with good. Rom. 12:20, 21.

Finally, that we are to do good in all respects, "commending ourselves to every man's conscience in the sight of God," and according to the law of Christ, do nothing to others that we would not wish them to do unto us. 2 Cor. 4:2; Matt. 7:12; Luke 6:31.

Article XV.

The Swearing of Oaths.

Regarding the swearing of oaths, we believe and confess, that the Lord Jesus has dissuaded his followers from and forbidden them the same; that is, that he commanded them to "swear not at all;" but that their "Yea" should be "yea," and their "Nay, nay." From which we understand that all oaths, high and low, are forbidden; and that instead of them we are to confirm all our promises and covenants, declarations and testimonies of all matters, merely with "Yea that is yea," and "Nay that is nay;" and that we are to perform and fulfill at all times, and in all things, to every one, every promise and obligation to which we thus affirm, as faithfully as if we had confirmed it by the most solemn oath. And if we thus do, we have the confidence that no one —not even government itself—will have just cause to require more of us. Matt. 5:34—37; James 5:12; 2 Cor. 1:17.

Article XVI.

Excommunication or Expulsion from the Church.

We also believe in and acknowledge the ban, or excommunication, a separation or spiritual punishment by the church, for the amendment, and not for the destruction, of offenders; so that what is pure may be separated from that which is impure. That is, if a person, after having been enlightened, and received the knowledge of the truth, and has been received into the communion of the saints, does willfully, or out of presumption, sin against God, or commit some other "sin unto death," thereby falling into such unfruitful works of darkness, that he becomes separated from God, and is debarred from his kingdom—that such an one—when his works are become manifest, and sufficiently known to the church—cannot remain in the "congregation of the righteous;" but must, as an offensive member and open sinner, be excluded from the church, "rebuked before all," and "purged out as a leaven," and thus remain until his amendment, as an example and warning to others, and also that the church may be kept pure from such "spots" and "blemishes;" so that not for the want of this, the name of the Lord be blasphemed, the church dishonored, and a stumbling-block thrown in the way of those "without," and finally, that the offender may not be condemned with the world, but that he may again be convinced of the error of his ways, and brought to repentance and amendment of life. Isaiah 59:2; 1 Cor. 5:5, 6, 12; 1 Tim. 5:20; 2 Cor. 13:10.

Regarding the brotherly admonition, as also the instruction of the erring, we are to "give all diligence" to watch over them, and exhort them in all meekness to the amendment of their ways (James 5:19, 20); and in case any should remain obstinate and unconverted, to reprove them as the case may require. In short, the church must "put away from among herself him that is wicked," whether it be in doctrine or life.

Article XVII.
The Shunning of Those Who are Expelled.

As regards the withdrawing from, or the shunning of, those who are expelled, we believe and confess, that if any one, whether it be through a wicked life or perverse doctrine—is so far fallen as to be separated from God, and consequently rebuked by, and expelled from, the church, he must also, according to the doctrine of Christ and his apostles, be shunned and avoided by all the members of the church (particularly by those to whom his misdeeds are known), whether it be in eating or drinking, or other such like social matters. In short, that we are to have nothing to do with him; so that we may not become defiled by intercourse with him, and partakers of his sins; but that he may be made ashamed, be affected in his mind, convinced in his conscience, and thereby induced to amend his ways. 1 Cor. 5:9—11; Rom. 16:17; 2 Thess. 3:14; Tit. 3:10.

That nevertheless, as well in shunning as in reproving such offender, such moderation and christian discretion be used, that such shunning and reproof may not be conducive to his ruin, but be serviceable to his amendment. For should he be in need, hungry, thirsty, naked, sick or visited by some other affliction, we are in duty bound, according to the doctrine and practice of Christ and his apostles, to render him aid and assistance, as necessity may require; otherwise the shunning of him might be rather conducive to his ruin than to his amendment. 1 Thess. 5:14.

Therefore we must not treat such offenders as enemies, but exhort them as brethren, in order thereby to bring them to a knowledge of their sins and to repentance; so that they may again become reconciled to God and the church, and be received and admitted into the same—thus exercising love towards them, as is becoming. 2 Thess. 3:15.

Article XVIII.

The Resurrection of the Dead and the Last Judgment.

Regarding the resurrection of the dead, we confess with the mouth, and believe with the heart, that according to the scriptures—all men who shall have died or "fallen asleep," will—through the incomprehensible power of God—at the day of judgment, be "raised up" and made alive; and that these, together with all those who then remain alive, and who shall be "changed in a moment, in the twinkling of an eye, at the last trump," shall "appear before the judgment-seat of Christ," where the good shall be separated from the evil, and where "every one shall receive the things done in his body, according to that he hath done, whether it be good or bad;" and that the good or pious shall then further, as the blessed of their Father, be received by Christ into eternal life, where they shall receive that joy which "eye hath not seen, nor ear heard, nor hath entered into the heart of man." Yea, where they shall reign and triumph with Christ forever and ever. Matt. 22:30, 31; 25:31; Dan. 12:2; Job 19:25, 26; John 5:28, 29; 1 Cor. 15; 1 Thess. 4:13.

And that, on the contrary, the wicked or impious, shall, as the accursed of God, be cast into "outer darkness;" yea, into eternal, hellish torments; "where their worm dieth not, and the fire is not quenched;" and where—according to Holy Scripture—they can expect no comfort nor redemption throughout eternity. Isaiah 66:24; Matt. 25:46; Mark 9:46; Rev. 14:11.

May the Lord through his grace make us all fit and worthy, that no such calamity may befall any of us; but that we may be diligent, and so take heed to ourselves, that we may be found of him in peace, without spot, and blameless. Amen.

Now these are, as before mentioned, the chief articles of our general Christian Faith, which we every where teach in our congregations and families, and according to which we profess to live; and which, according to our convictions, contain the only true Christian Faith, which the apostles in their time believed and taught; yea, which they testified to by their lives and confirmed by their deaths; in which we will also, according to our weakness, gladly abide, live, and die, that at last, together with the apostles and all the pious we may obtain the salvation of our souls through the grace of God.

Thus were the foregoing articles of faith adopted and concluded by our united churches in the city of Dort, in Holland, on the 21st day of April, in the year of our Lord 1632, and signed by the following ministers and teachers.

DORT.
Isaac Koenig,
Johann Cobryssen,
Jan Jacobs,
Jacuis Terwen,
Claes Dirksen,
Mels Gysbaerts,
Adrian Cornelis.

FLISSINGEN.
Dillaert Willeborts,
Jacob Pennen,
Lieven Marymehr.

AMSTERDAM.
Tobias Goverts,
Peter Jansen Mayer,
Abram Dirks,
David ter Haer,
Peter Jan von Zingel.

MIDDLEBURG.
Bastian Willemsen,
Jan Winkelmans.

HARLEM
John Doom,
Peter Gryspeer,
Dirk Wouters Kolenkamp,
Peter Joosten.

BOMMEL.
Wilhelm Jan von Exselt,
Gispert Spiering.

ROTTERDAM.
Balten Centen Schumacher,
Michael Michiels,
Israel von Halmael,
Heinrich Dirkse Apeldoren,
Andreas Lucken.

SCHIEDAM.
Cornelis Bom,
Lambrecht Paeldink.

LEYDEN.
Christian de Kopink,
Jan Weyns.

BLOCKZYL.
Claes Claesson,
Peter Peterson.

ZIRICZEE.
Anton Cornelis,
Peter Jan Zimmerman.

UTRECHT.
Herman Segers,
Jan Heinrich Hochfeld,
Daniel Horens,
Abraham Spronk,
Wilhelm von Brockhuysen.

FROM THE UPPER COUNTRY.
Peter von Borsel,
Anton Hans.

CREVELDT.
Herman op den Graff,
Wilhelm Kreynen.

ZEALAND.
Cornelis de Moir,
Isaac Claes.

GORCUM.
Jacob von Sebrecht,
Jan J. von Kruysen.

ARNHEIM.
Cornelis Jans,
Dirk Renderson.

Besides this confession being adopted by so many churches, and signed by their ministers, all the churches in Alsace and Germany afterwards adopted it unanimously. Wherefore it was translated from the Holland into the languages of these countries—into French and German—for the use of the churches there, and for others. Of which this may serve as a notice.

The following attestation was signed by the brethren in Alsace, who examined this confession and adopted it as their own.

We, the undersigned, ministers of the word of God, and elders of the church in Alsace, hereby declare and make known, that being assembled this 4th of Feb. in the year of our Lord 1660, at Onenheim, on account of the Confession of Faith, which was adopted at the Peace Convention in the city of Dort, on the 21st day of April in the year 1632; and having examined the same, and found it, according to our judgment, in agreement with the word of God, we have entirely adopted it as our own. Which we, in testimony of the truth, and a firm faith, have signed with our own hands, as follows:

MINISTERS.

MAGENHEIM.
John Miller.
HEIDELHEIM.
John Ringer.
BALDENHEIM.
Jacob Schebly.
ISENHEIM.
Henry Schneider.
KUNENHEIM.
Rudolph Egli.
MARKIRCH.
Adolph Schmidt.

ELDERS.

MARKIRCH.
Jacob Schmidt,
Bertram Habich.
OHNENHEIM.
Ulrich Husser.
Jacob Gochnauer.
JEPSENHEIM.
John Rudolph Bumen.
DUERRSANZENHEIM.
Jacob Schneider.
KUNENHEIM.
Henry Frick.

POSTSCRIPT TO THE FOREGOING 18 ARTICLES.

From an authentic circular letter of the year 1557, from the Highland to the Netherland churches, it appears that from the Eyfelt to Moravia there were 50 churches, of which some consisted of from 500 to 600 brethren. And that there were about that time, at a conference at Strasburg, about 50 preachers and elders present, who discoursed about matters concerning the welfare of the churches.

These leaders of the non-resistant Christians endeavored earnestly to propagate the truth; so that like a "grain of mustard seed," of small beginning, it grew against all bloody persecution, to the height in which it is to be seen in so many large churches in Germany, Prussia, the Principality of Cleves, &c., and particularly in the United Netherlands.

But finally, alas! there arose disunion amongst them about matters of faith, which so deeply grieved the peaceably disposed amongst them, that they not only thought about means to heal the schism, and restore union, but did also take the matter in hand, and concluded at Cologne, in the year 1591, a laudable peace between the Highland and Netherland churches. Still th schism was not fully healed. Consequently in the years 1628 and 1630, it was deemed necessary at a certain conference, by some lovers of peace to appoint another conference, in order to see whether they could come to an understanding, and the schism be fully healed. Consequently, in order to attain this object in the most effectual manner, there assembled at Dort, from many of the churches in Holland, on the 21st of April, 1632, fifty-one ministers of the word of God, appointed for said purpose; who deemed it advisable that a scriptural confession of faith should be drawn up, to which all parties should adhere, and on which this peace convention and the intended union should be founded and built. Which was then accordingly drawn up, publicly adopted, confirmed, signed, the so much wished for peace obtained, and the light again put on the candlestick, to the honor of the non-resistant Christianity.

The Shorter Catechism.

Brief Instruction from Holy Scripture, in Questions and Answers, for the Young.

The following questions and answers, contain in brief, the principal doctrines of our faith, and are designed for the instruction of those who desire to unite with the church.

Ques. 1. What prompts you to desire to unite with the communion of believers, and be baptized?

Ans. I am impelled by faith, to separate myself from the world and its sinful lusts, and to submit myself in obedience to my Lord, Redeemer and Savior, for the salvation of my soul. Heb. 5:9.

Ques. What has induced you to this?

Ans. The will and good pleasure of God, which were proclaimed and demonstrated to me through the preaching of the holy gospel, in which were also revealed unto me the laws and commandments of Christ; which I am bound to receive and observe in true faith? Matt. 7:21; 19:17.

Ques. 3. Do you then expect to be justified and saved through your good works, and the keeping of the commandments of Christ?

Ans. No. For through our good works alone we cannot merit heaven; for salvation is the unmerited grace of God purchased for us by Jesus Christ. Eph. 2:8.

Ques. 4. For what purpose are then good works or the keeping of the commandments of Christ necessary?

Ans. They are evidence of true faith in Jesus Christ; for obedience from love to God, is the light and life of faith, without which, "faith is dead." James 2:20.

Ques. 5. Through what is man justified before God?

Ans. Through the Lord Jesus Christ alone; of whose righteousness we must become partakers through "faith which worketh by love." Gal. 5:6.

Ques. 6. What is true faith?

Ans. It is a certain knowledge, whereby we hold every thing as true that is revealed to us in the Holy Scriptures; and whereby we cherish a full confidence, that the pardon of our sins, righteousness, and eternal life, are granted unto us by God, through our Lord Jesus Christ. Eph. 2:5.

Ques. 7. What do you believe?

Ans. I believe in God, Father, Son, and Holy Ghost.

Ques. 8. How do you believe in God the Father?

Ans. I believe with the heart, and confess with the mouth, that He is one, eternal, almighty, and just God, the Creator and Preserver of heaven and earth, together with all things visible and invisible. Gen 14:17.

Ques. 9. How do you believe in the Son?

Ans. I believe that he is Jesus Christ, the Son of the living God, our Savior and Redeemer, who has been with the Father from eternity, and who, in the "fullness of time," was sent into the world; that he was conceived by the Holy Ghost, born of the blessed Virgin Mary, suffered for us under Pontius Pilate, was crucified, died, and was buried; rose again from the dead on the third day, ascended into heaven, and sits at the right hand of God, the Almighty Father: whence he will again come to judge the living and the dead. Matt. 25:31; John 17:5; Gal. 4:4.

Ques. 10. How do you believe in the Holy Ghost?

Ans. I believe and confess, that the Holy Ghost proceedeth from the Father and the Son, and is of a divine nature; therefore I also believe in God, Father, Son, and Holy Ghost, as being one true God. Besides I also confess a general Holy Christian Church, the communion of Saints, the forgiveness of sins, the resurrection of the flesh, and thereafter eternal life. 1 John 5:20; John 5:29.

Ques. 11. What do you confess of the Christian Church, or the Congregation of the Lord?

Ans. I confess by my faith, that there is a Church of God, which the Lord Jesus purchased with his own blood, and which he "sanctified and cleansed with the washing of water by the word, that he might present it to himself a glorious church." Eph. 5:26, 27.

Ques. 12. In what does the Church of God consist?

Ans. In a number of persons, who, through faith in Jesus Christ, have withdrawn from the sinful world, and submitted in obedience to the gospel, not to live any more to themselves, but to Christ in true humility; who also "give diligence" to exercise christian virtues, by observing God's holy ordinances. Such are members of the body of Christ, and heirs of eternal life. 2 Pet. 1:11.

Ques. 13. How, and through what, is the Church of God maintained?

Ans. Through the preaching of the holy gospel, and the teaching of the Holy Ghost, for the purpose of carrying on and maintaining which, teachers and ministers are elected by the church. Eph. 4:11.

Ques. 14. Who has given power to the church to choose teachers?

Ans. I confess that according to the practice of the disciples, so has God also given authority to his church to do; namely to elect teachers and ministers, that the "body of Christ may be edified" and preserved. Wherefore the election of such teachers and ministers also takes place according to the example which the apostles were accustomed to observe in such matters. Eph. 4:12; Acts 1:15—26.

Ques. 15. Whence comes the ordinance of the service to the poor?

Ans. Of this service we have an example in the Acts of the Apostles; who, when the "number of the disciples was multiplied," called together the multitude, and caused to be "appointed from among them, seven men," who took charge of such "business," which example is still observed; so that *that which* is contributed by christian hearts, is properly applied to the relief of the necessities of the poor members of the church. Acts 6:1; Eph. 4:28.

Ques. 16. How and through what means are the members of the body of Christ incorporated into the church?

Ans. Through the ordinance of christian baptism, on confession of their faith, and repentance of their past sins; whereupon they are baptized in the name of the Father, the Son, and the Holy Ghost. Matt. 28:19.

Ques. 17. What is baptism properly?

Ans. I confess that it is an external ordinance of Christ, a sign of a spiritual birth from God, a "putting on of Christ," and an incorporation into his church, an evidence that we have established a covenant with Christ? Rom. 6:4; Gal. 3:27; 1 Pet. 3:21.

Ques. 18. Of what use is baptism?

Ans. It represents to true believers the washing away of the impurity of their souls, through the blood of Christ, namely, the pardon of their sins; whereupon they console themselves with the hope of eternal salvation, through Jesus Christ, whom they have "put on" in baptism. Gal. 3:27.

Ques. 19. To what are the members of the church of Christ, obligated by baptism?

Ans. To the act of burying their past sins into Christ's death and of binding themselves to Christ in a new life and conversation—a life of obedience—in order that they may follow his will, and do what he has commanded them. Matt. 28:20.

Ques. 20. What is the Lord's Supper?

Ans. I confess that it is an external ceremony and institution of Christ, administered to believers in the form of bread and wine; in the partaking of which, the death and sufferings of Christ are to be declared and observed to his memory. 1 Cor. 11:26.

Ques. 21. What purpose does the observance of the Lord's Supper subserve?

Ans. It is thereby represented to us, how Christ's holy body was sacrificed on the cross, and his precious blood shed for us—for the pardon of our sins. 1 John, 1:7.

Ques. 22. What is the use of the observance of the Lord's Supper?

Ans. We thereby bear witness to our simple obedience to Christ, our Savior and Redeemer, which has the promise of eternal salvation. Further, it secures unto us, through faith, the communion of the body and blood of Christ, and comforts us with the benefit of his death; that is, the assurance of the pardon of our sins. 1 Cor. 10:16; Heb. 5:9.

Ques. 23. Is marriage also an institution of God?

Ans. Yes. For it is instituted by God himself, and confirmed in the case of Adam and Eve in the Garden of Eden. Gen. 1:27, 28.

Ques. 24. For what purpose is marriage instituted?

Ans. For the purpose of preserving the human race, so that the earth may thereby be peopled with inhabitants, and that fornication be avoided. Therefore "every man" is to "have his own wife," and "every woman her own husband." 1 Cor. 7:2.

Ques. 25. How must such marriage be begun, so that it does not conflict with the institution?

Ans. Persons who are not too nearly related by consanguinity, may, after diligent prayer to God, enter into this state, and endeavor to live therein, in a Christian manner to the end of their days; provided that they—as members of the Christian Church—enter into marriage only with members of the church. Lev. 18:6—17; 1 Cor. 7:39; 9:5.

Ques. 26. Is a member of the church not at all allowed to enter into matrimony with a person who is not agreed with him in faith and doctrine?

Ans. No. For this is contrary to the marriage institution; and he who thus enters into matrimony, acts contrary to the law of God, and the doctrine of the apostles. Deut. 7:3, 4; Judges 3:6, 7; 1 Cor. 1:10; 7:39; Phil. 2:1, 2.

Ques. 27. Can also a lawful marriage, for any cause be divorced?

Ans. No. For the persons united by such marriage are so closely bound to each other, that they can in no wise separate, except in case of "fornication." Matt. 19:9.

Ques. 28. What do you confess in regard to the power of civil government?

Ans. I confess, from the testimony of Holy Scripture, that kings and governments are instituted by God, for the welfare and common interest of the countries over which they rule; and that he who resists such authorities, "resists the ordinance of God." Rom. 13:1. Wherefore we are under obligation to fear and honor government, and obey the same in all things that do not militate against the word of God. So we are also commanded to pray for the same. 1. Tim. 1:2.

Ques. 29. Is it allowed to swear an oath?

Ans. No. For although this was allowed to the fathers of the Old Testament, yet has our Lord and institutor of the New Testament, Christ Jesus, expressly forbidden it (Matt. 5:33—37), which is confirmed by the apostle James, when he says: "Above all things, my brethren, swear not; but let your Yea be yea; and your Nay, nay; lest ye fall into condemnation." James 5:12.

Ques. 30. Is it allowed to take revenge?

Ans. No: although there was liberty to do so under the Old Testament Dispensation. But now that it is totally forbidden by Christ and his apostles, we must not lust after it, but in meekness do good unto our neighbor; yea, also, to our enemies. Matt. 5:38, 39; Rom. 12:19-21.

Ques. 31. If a member of the church fall into some sin, or misdeed, what is to be done in such case?

Ans. I confess by virtue of the doctrine of Christ and his apostles, that reproof and discipline must be fostered and maintained amongst believers; so that the headstrong, as well as such as have committed gross sins and works of the flesh—whereby they have separated themselves from God—may not be suffered in the communion of believers; but for their own amendment, be "rebuked before all, that others also may fear." Matt. 18:15—18; Isa. 59:2; 1 Tim. 5:20.

Ques. 32. How must we conduct ourselves towards such as are thus separated from the church?

Ans. According to the doctrine of the apostles, the true members of the church of Christ are to withdraw from such reproved and impenitent offenders, and have no spiritual communion with them, except by chance or occasion, when they may be exhorted in love, compassion, and Christian discretion, again to rise from their fallen state, and return to the church. Rom. 16:17; Tit. 3:10.

Ques. 33. How long is the avoiding of such offenders to be observed?

Ans. Until they return, give evidence of repentance — of sorrow for their sins — and earnestly desire again to be admitted into the communion of the church. In such case they are, after solemn prayer to God, again received and admitted into the church. 2 Cor. 2:6, 7.

Ques. 34. What do you believe concerning the second coming of Christ, and the resurrection of the dead?

Ans. I believe that Christ, our Head, Lord, and Savior will—just as he visibly ascended to heaven—again appear from thence in great power and glory, "with a shout, and with the trump of God." 1 Thess. 4:16. "For the hour is coming, in the which all that are in their graves shall hear his voice, and shall come forth; they that have done good, unto the resurrection of life; and they that have done evil, unto the resurrection of damnation." John 5:28, 29. "For we must all appear before the judgment seat of Christ; that every one may receive the things done in his body, according to that he hath done, whether it be good or bad." 2 Cor. 5:10.

Ques. 35. Now as this confession agrees with the doctrine of Christ and his apostles: Are you inclined with all your heart, to submit yourself to the will of your Redeemer and Savior, Jesus Christ—to deny yourself, together with all sinful lusts—and to strive by the grace of God, in true faith and heart-felt humility—to lead a pious and godly life and holy conversation, according to the commandments of God as long as you live?

Ans. I am.

The minister then wishes the young disciple the rich blessing and grace of God, through the power of the Holy Spirit unto salvation. To him be honor and praise for ever and ever. Amen.

Ministers Manual.

THE ADMINISTRATION OF BAPTISM.

When any person, by the grace of God, has come to a saving knowledge of the truth, and desires to enter into a covenant with God to be baptized and received into church membership, he should make known his desire to the bishop or ministers, or to any member of the church, who may inform the minister. The bishop or minister then inquires of the applicant whether he believes that his desire to live a better life is a call from God to the saving of his soul; whether he realizes that he himself is not able to do any part of the saving work, and that it is impossible for him of his own will to continue faithful in the good work begun in his heart; whether he believes that God, of his own grace and power, will, upon true repentance, forgive him his sins, give him a new heart, adopt him into the family of God, and receive him into the fellowship of the saints. Also whether he is willing to submit himself to the Gospel of Jesus

Christ and his non-resistant doctrine, in all things to be advised and instructed by the word of God; whether he is at peace with his neighbors and fellowmen generally, so far as it is possible, and whether he is connected with any secret society, or is in any other way living contrary to the teachings of the Gospel as we interpret it, and if so, whether he is willing unconditionally to withdraw from any such secret organization, and in every respect to renounce all the errors of his former life. If the applicant gives satisfactory evidence that he is prompted by the Spirit of God, and is willing to conform to the requirements of the Gospel, the bishop or minister publishes the request before the Congregation, and admonishes the members to observe the walk and conduct of the applicant, to show him a good example in a pious spiritual life, and to pray for him.

The subject or subjects (if more than one) for baptism should then be well instructed in the doctrines of repentance, forgiveness of sins, regeneration, the life of God in the soul, the ordinances to be observed, the restrictions which the Gospel places upon the Christian, and the rules of church government. The meetings for this purpose may be held at the meeting-house or at some other convenient place, on the afternoon of each meeting day, or any other appropriate time and place may be selected. The minister should give such instructions on the above mentioned subjects and others, as he may consider suitable and necessary. The converts should be instructed to read and study carefully the eighteen articles of our confession of faith, and the minister should make it his duty to see that they understand them. They should also be made acquainted with the rules and requirements of the church, as well as the duties which church-membership imposes upon them, and the privileges it bestows.

The object of these instructions is to edify and confirm the subjects for baptism in their faith, and encourage them to persevere in the right way. All applicants for baptism and admission into the church should be able to give satisfactory evidence that they have truly repented of their sins, and have found peace in their souls through faith in Jesus Christ, and that they have passed from death unto life.

At least three or four of these meetings should be held before baptism. In some places they are held much oftener. These should be opened and closed with prayer, and if practicable, with the singing of a hymn. In many places the instruction meetings are held publicly, the members and the congregation in general, being present, which is appropriate and profitable for both the members and the unconverted.

In some localities, before baptism is administered, a counsel of the church is held for the purpose of ascertaining whether there is any scriptural reason to prevent the admission of any of the applicants into the church. If no cause is found, they are requested to meet again on the day preceding baptism, upon which occasion the eighteen articles of the confession are read to them and explained, and they are asked whether they believe in and fully agree with these doctrines. If they answer in the affirmative, they are exhorted to stand firm, and be faithful in the commandments of God, and to continue in good works unto the end.

In other places the names of the applicants are simply published in the meeting, and if no objection is presented, and the candidates have been sufficiently instructed, either publicly or privately, the time for baptism is appointed, and the exercises are proceeded with as follows:

After singing a hymn, the minister or deacon may appropriately read John 1:1—36. After the usual opening services and prayer, the bishop or another minister takes an appropriate text, and preaches a discourse from it (observing not to preach too long).

He then descends from the desk, and says to the congregation: When our dear Lord and Savior Jesus Christ, gave his last commission to his disciples he said: "All power is given unto me, in heaven and in earth. Go ye therefore and teach all nations, baptizing them in the name of the Father, and of the Son, and of the Holy Ghost, teaching them to observe all things whatsoever I have commanded you." And again: "Go ye into all the world and preach the gospel to every creature; he that believeth and is baptized shall be saved; but he that believeth not shall be damned." In accordance with these declarations of the word of God, these dear souls have presented themselves before us for the purpose of being baptized, and thus making a covenant with God, and being received into the communion and fellowship of the church.

They have been instructed in the doctrines of the gospel and in the ordinances and requirements of the church, and have given evidence that they are prompted in their purpose by the Spirit of God, that they are willing to forsake sin and the world, to consecrate themselves to the service of God, and from henceforth to be the disciples and followers of Christ. As we now are witnesses of these solemn exercises, let each one of us remember our own covenant and pray that the solemn promises which shall be made here to-day, before God and this congregation, may be made in all sincerity, and that God may bless and establish these dear souls in his grace, that they may be strong in the Lord, zealous in good works, ornaments in the Christian profession, shining lights in the world, and faithful in all things unto the end. And as there is joy in heaven over one sinner that repenteth, so let our hearts rejoice that God has led these precious souls to turn from their former ways and come into the fold of Christ. As we thus rejoice let us likewise pray that God may lead yet many more to follow their good example. Amen.

Addressing the applicants, the minister says: And now if it is still your desire to be baptized and to be received into church fellowship, you will arise.

He then addresses to the applicants the following questions:

1. Do you believe in one true, eternal, and almighty God, who is the Creator and Preserver of all visible and invisible things?

Answer: I do.

2. Do you believe in Jesus Christ, as the only begotten Son of God, that he is the only Savior of mankind, that he died upon the cross, and gave himself a ransom for our sins, that through him we might have eternal life?

Answer: I do.

3. Do you believe in the Holy Ghost which proceedeth from the Father and the Son; that he is an abiding Comforter, sanctifies the hearts of men, and guides them into all truth?

Answer: I do.

(NOTE.—The foregoing questions are, by some, combined in one; but it is better to ask them separately, in order that they may be better understood.)

4. Are you truly sorry for your past sins, and are you willing to renounce Satan, the world, and all works of darkness and your own carnal will and sinful desires?
Answer: I am.

5. Do you promise by the grace of God, and the aid of his Holy Spirit, to submit yourself to Christ and his word, and faithfully to abide in the same until death?
Answer: I do.

After these questions have been asked and answered affirmatively, the minister and the subjects for baptism kneel, while the congregation stands, and the minister prays for God's blessing upon them, that they may have grace to remain steadfast and be faithful to the end in the promises they have made.

After prayer, the minister arises, while the subjects for baptism remain kneeling. The deacon or some other brother now brings a vessel with water, and the minister laying his hands upon the head of the subject for baptism, says: "Upon the confession of thy faith, which thou hast made before God and these witnesses (He now with both hands takes a quantity of water from the vessel, and pours it upon the head of the applicant), I baptize thee in the name of the Father, and of the Son, and of the Holy Ghost."*

After all the applicants are thus baptized, the minister returns to the one first baptized, and taking him by the hand, says:

"In the name of Christ and his church, I give you my hand: Arise! and as Christ was raised up by the glory of the Father, even so thou also shalt walk in newness of life, and so long as thou art faithful and abidest in the doctrine of his word, thou art his disciple indeed, and shalt be acknowledged as a member of the body of Christ, and a brother (or sister) in the church." He then gives him the kiss of peace and says: "The Lord bless thee and keep thee. Amen."

In the same manner he also raises the female converts, and the wife of the minister or deacon, or any sister in the church, gives them the kiss of peace, and thus receives them into the fellowship of the church.

---

* Some, instead of, "Which thou hast made before God and these witnesses," say, "repentance and sorrow for thy sins," etc.

The minister now takes his place again at the desk, and gives such further instructions as he may deem necessary, after which the services are closed in the usual manner.

If any person who has been connected with another denomination, and having been baptized upon the confession of his faith*, wishes to unite with the church, he is not rebaptized, unless he earnestly desires it, but is taught the doctrines of the Bible, and the rules of order as we believe and practice them. If he agrees with these, and the church has no cause against him, the minister, in the presence of the whole congregation asks him the following questions:

"Do you confess that you are of the same mind with us in the doctrines and rules of the church; and do you promise to remain faithful and obedient in the same until death?" If he answers this affirmatively, the minister takes him by the hand, saying: "Upon this confession which thou hast made before God and these witnesses, thou shalt be acknowledged as a brother (or sister) in the church; and so long as thou art faithful and abidest in the doctrine of

---

* Persons who were baptized in their infancy, cannot be received into the church without being rebaptized.

his Word, thou art his disciple indeed." The kiss of peace is then given, and he says: "The Lord bless thee and keep thee. Amen."

Frequently applicants prefer to be baptized in the water. In this case the questions are sometimes asked, and the prayer offered in the house. The services here may be closed by the singing of a hymn before proceeding to the water. Here the minister, standing with the converts near the water, surrounded by the congregation, reads Acts 8:35—39, or some other short and appropriate Scripture. He may also add, as circumstances may suggest, a few words of comment or admonition, or the congregation may sing a hymn. The minister then leads the applicants, one or two at a time, into the water, where the applicants kneel and the minister takes up water with both hands, pours it on their heads, and proceeds further as described above.

EXAMINATION PRECEDING THE COMMUNION OF THE LORD'S SUPPER.

Self-examination is a duty enjoined upon all Christian believers. We read, "Let us search and try our ways, and turn again to the Lord." Lam. 3:40. "Let a man examine himself, and so let him eat of that bread and drink of that cup," 1 Cor. 11:28. "Examine yourselves, whether ye be in the faith; prove your own selves." 2 Cor. 13:5. "Purge out therefore the old leaven, that ye may be a new lump, as ye are unleavened." 1 Cor. 5:7. "Put away from among yourselves that wicked person," etc. 1 Cor. 5:13.

Hence it is the custom of the church, several weeks before the communion of the Lord's Supper is observed, to hold a church examination, for the purpose of obtaining a knowledge of the standing and condition of each member.

When the day for the examination meeting is made known to the church, the minister should admonish the membership to improve the time to their spiritual benefit, to endeavor by prayer, meditation and the reading of the Scriptures, to come especially near to God, to purge out the old leaven of sin and impurity that might yet beset them, that they may gain new strength to walk in love, meekness, humility, and self-denial, according to the example of Jesus; and further, if any one has aught against his neighbor or brother, or is aware that his neighbor or brother has aught against him, that he go to him, and deal with him according to the instructions of our Savior given in Matt. 5:23, 24, and 18:15, 35, and thus earnestly, kindly and sincerely seek a reconciliation, so that all may be duly prepared for the solemn occasion.

At the time of the examination, the minister or ministers (if more than one is present), with the deacons, retire to the counsel-room, where the members, one by one, present themselves, and in some churches extend to the minister the right hand as a token of peace. Then the minister asks: "Do you acknowledge peace with God, with the church, and with all men; and is it your desire to partake of the communion of the Lord's Supper?"

Should any one offer any complaint against any brother or sister, before he has observed the rule given in Matt. 18:15—16, his complaint cannot under any circumstances be received, unless it be a flagrant transgression. (The minister who receives a complaint in a case where the complainant has not observed the above rule, makes himself liable to censure). But when this rule has been observed, and every effort to win him has failed, the complaint will be received, and the transgressor will be further dealt with according to the same rule.

After all the brethren and sisters have thus presented themselves, the ministers return to the audience room, and report to the brotherhood the result of the examination, and usually announce the time when the communion of the Lord's Supper will be observed.

NOTE 1. While the examination is progressing, the congregation may very appropriately spend the time in singing.

NOTE 2. In case that any of the brethren or sisters do not attend the examination meeting, they should be visited by the minister or deacon before communion. If any dissatisfaction exists, an effort should be made to bring about a reconciliation, so that with each communion, all difficulties and dissatisfactions throughout the district may be adjusted, and thus the peace and harmony, as well as the purity of the church preserved.

Note 3. The examination meeting before communion is a custom in our church which is founded upon the teachings of Christ and his apostles, as we have shown above, and should never be omitted, in order that the church may be preserved pure, and that such as are unworthy and walk not in accordance with the teachings and example of Christ may be made manifest, and not impose themselves upon the church and partake of the communion, and thus bring reproach upon the people of God. "Know ye not that a little leaven leaveneth the whole lump." 1 Cor. 5:6.

THE COMMUNION OF THE LORD'S SUPPER.

The Lord's Supper is usually observed in the Spring and fall of each year. The meeting on this occasion is opened by singing an appropriate hymn, after which the 26th chapter of Matthew or the 22d chapter of Luke or some other appropriate Scripture is read. One of the ministers then delivers a short address, in which he points out the importance and solemnity of the occasion, and then offers a prayer.

After prayer, a suitable text is read, and the bishop or another minister preaches a discourse appropriate to the occasion. The object of the communion is generally presented, showing that the eating and drinking together of the members of the church, at the Lord's table, is expressive of the communion and unity of the church as "the body of Christ." Also the great love of Jesus, which he manifested toward us as our Savior, his sufferings and death upon the cross, the great salvation which he, through his suffering, wrought for us and how he instituted in commemoration thereof, his Holy Supper, and commanded all his true followers to observe and keep the same.

When the discourse is concluded, the bishop usually reads 1 Cor. 11:23—29, and again exhorts the congregation to self-examination, after which the bread (the bread and wine should be placed on the table at the opening of the meeting, and remain covered until the bishop is ready to use them) is placed before the bishop by the deacon, the bread being cut into long 'slices. The bishop takes the bread and gives thanks, the congregation the while standing. After the congregation is again seated,* the minister breaks the bread, and gives to each communicant as he rises to his feet to receive it, a piece, until all are served.†

During the distribution of the bread, the bishop repeats the words of our Savior given

---

* In some congregations the members remain standing until they are served.

† It has been the custom with many of our ministers to partake of the bread and wine before offering it to any of the members, but in later years, many prefer to receive it from one of their fellow ministers after a part or all the others have been served.

in Luke 22:19. "This is my body which is given for you; this do in remembrance of me," or 1 Cor. 10:16, "The bread which we brake is it not the communion of the body of Christ," or 1 Cor. 11:24, "Take, eat, this is my body," etc., or some other appropriate text or benediction.

In some parts of the country, the minister stands by the table, or in some convenient place, and those wishing to partake of the Supper, rise from their seats and go to him to receive the bread, and afterwards the wine, while in other localities, the minister proceeds through the house from seat to seat, while the communicant, as stated above, simply rises to his feet to receive it.

After all the members have been served with bread, the deacon pours the wine into the cup. The congregation again rise, and the minister takes the cup and gives thanks, after which he hands it to each individual communicant after the same manner in which he distributed the bread, repeating meanwhile the words, "This cup is the New Testament in my blood, which is shed for you," Luke 22:20; or, "The cup of blessing which we bless, is it not the communion of the blood of Christ?" 1 Cor. 10:16; "This cup is the New Testament in my blood: this do ye, as oft as ye drink it, in remembrance of me. For as often as ye eat this bread, and drink this cup, ye do shew the Lord's death till he come," 1 Cor. 11:25, 26, or some other appropriate text.

After all the members have partaken of the cup, the minister briefly admonishes the congregation to remain faithful in the service of God, walk humbly, and exercise meekness and love toward all men, and then closes the meeting in the usual manner, by offering a prayer, singing a hymn, and the benediction.

FEET-WASHING.

With the benediction the congregation in general is dismissed.* But those who have partaken of the communion of the Lord's Supper, remain to take part in the exercise of feet-washing, which is performed immediately after the communion. Any, however, who wish to remain to witness the ceremony, are always welcome to do so. The bishop or another minister reads from John 13:1—17, and then makes some remarks showing that this act of humility was instituted by our Savior; that he commanded his disciples to do one to another as he had done to them; and that by this blessed example we should, by a willing obedience to this command, be prompted to declare our love both towards him and the brethren. Also that it shows the relation which the members of the "body of Christ" sustain to one another, Christ being Lord and Master, and yet doing the work of a servant, thereby showing that the church

---

* In some places the congregation is not dismissed until feet-washing is concluded, which in many instances is preferable.

is a brotherhood in which each member stands upon the same equality with the others, all being brethren in Christ, willing, even as our Savior, to perform to the glory of God, the most menial and common service, sincerely considering how his dear Son humbled himself, and with his own precious blood washed our souls from sin, purified our hearts, and redeemed us from everlasting death.

The deacons now bring vessels with water, and the two sexes, each among themselves, wash one another's feet and wipe them with a towel, then giving each other the right hand, and the kiss of peace, upon which one of them says: "The Lord be with us, preserve us in peace, and strengthen us in love;" or some other words of greeting: The other responds: "Amen." Then two other brethren proceed in the same way, and so on until all have passed through this ceremony. The sisters proceed in the same manner.*

---

* In some localities the female members retire to the counsel room, with which almost every meeting-house is provided, and there wash another's feet, in the apartment by themselves. This is said by old ministers to have formerly been the general custom.

CHOOSING AND ORDAINING A MINISTER.

When a church is not fully provided with ministers, a brother is chosen from the congregation and ordained. The request is usually brought before conference, that the ordination may be made with the consent of conference and the approval of the church. As soon as convenient, the congregation is informed of the action of conference, and a day is appointed for the purpose of choosing a brother for the ministry. All the brethren and sisters are requested to be present. They are admonished to pray earnestly to God for his blessing upon their undertaking.

On the appointed day, the services are conducted as usual. The minister preaches a discourse appropriate to the occasion, in which he endeavors to impress the minds of the members with the importance of the duty before them, and shows them that, in the fear of God, according to their most solemn convictions, they should each cast their vote for the brother who they believe best fills the requirements which the Scriptures enjoin for this important work (1 Tim. 3:1—7) and whom they believe to be chosen of God.

The bishop now, with one or two fellow-ministers, retires to the counsel-room, and all the members who feel impressed to do so, one at a time, go in and mention the name of a brother who they are convinced in their hearts, has, according to the Scriptures, the necessary qualifications.* The name is written down. When all have given their voices, the ministers return to the audience room, and announce the name or names for which the votes were cast. If only one brother has been nominated, which is always desirable, the church has a united voice according to the instruction given in the Confession of Faith; and the brother thus chosen, after due examination, is ordained.†

---

* This is a work of solemn importance, that those who give their votes, should be fully convinced that the Spirit has revealed to them what they should do, and whom they should name. No one should venture upon this solemn duty thoughtlessly or carelessly.

† There are a number of congregations, especially among the Amish and Russian Mennonites, which choose their ministers by the voice of the members, con-

When more than one have received votes, the congregation is earnestly admonished again to commend the whole matter to God, and implore His help, and the direction of the Holy Spirit, that the choosing of one from this number may tend to the glory of God, and the well-being of the church.

A day is then appointed to choose by lot one from among those nominated. In the meantime the brethren named are examined and questioned regarding their faith, and are admonished to yield themselves in willing obedience into the hands of God. The meeting is opened as usual, and Luke 10 : 1—22 or some other appropriate Scripture is read. After prayer, the bishop delivers a discourse suitable to the occasion, and then reads Acts 1 : 23—26.

After the discourse, the deacons take as many books, of the same kind (as nearly alike as possible), as there are brethren to be chosen from, and retire to the counsel-room, where they place into one of the books the lot (a slip of pa-

---

sidering the one chosen who receives the highest number of votes. When two brethren receiving the highest number of votes, have received an equal number of votes, the lot is used to decide between them.

per on which is written, "The lot is cast into the lap; but the whole disposing thereof is of the Lord." Prov. 16:33, or, "Herewith God hath called thee to the ministry of the Gospel)."

The books are then taken into the audience-room, and placed on the desk or table. The bishop, with the whole congregation kneels in prayer, and commends the whole work to God, saying, along with other petitions: "Thou, Lord, which knowest the hearts of all men, show which of these thou hast chosen."

Each of the brethren nominated then takes a book, and the bishop proceeds to look for the lot. The one in whose book it is found is considered chosen, and is required to rise (in some congregations they kneel) and the bishop ordains him.

The bishop lays his hands upon his head and holds them there while he says:

"The Lord has called thee to preach the Gospel of Jesus Christ; to make known his holy word and the counsels of his will regarding our salvation. Go, preach the Gospel in its purity; admonish the unconverted to repent: instruct and encourage the church. Continue earnestly to read the word of God, to exhort and to teach.

Pray without ceasing; seek to be a faithful and zealous laborer in the vineyard of the Lord. Be instant in season and out of season, reprove, rebuke, exhort with all long-suffering and doctrine; continue in them; for in doing this, thou shalt both save thyself and those that hear thee. May the Lord direct, help, and bless thee. Amen."

The bishop then gives him his right hand and the kiss of peace. The other ministers also give him their hand and the kiss of peace, and wish God's aid and blessing upon his labors.

The bishop now admonishes the congregation to manifest in word and deed true Christian love to their newly ordained minister; to pray for him, and when he preaches the word, to be obedient thereto. The services are closed as usual.

CHOOSING AND ORDAINING A DEACON.*

The deacon is chosen from the congregation in the same manner as the minister. When the deacon is to be chosen, the bishop reads Acts 6:1—7, and shows what the duties of the deacon are. If more than one brother is nominated, the lot is cast as in the choosing of a minister. The brother chosen is asked to arise (or kneel), when the bishop lays his hands upon his head, and gives him the charge to his office as follows:

"It has pleased God to call thee to the office of deacon. It will now be your duty to receive, and take care of, the charities of the church, to distribute them to the needy members, according to their necessities; to visit the sick, the widows and the orphans, and comfort them and pray with them in their afflictions; also to assist

---

*In the Confession of Faith, according to the teachings of the apostle, there is provision made, also for the choosing and service of deaconesses, or female deacons. See art. 9, Con. of Faith. This custom however has long since passed into disuse and there are now, so far as we know, no deaconesses, in any of our churches.

the bishop in the administration of baptism, and the Lord's Supper; to bear testimony to the truth in their public ministrations, and, when from any reason no minister is present where the people meet for public worship, it will be your duty to conduct the services, by reading, exhortation and prayer. Where strife or difficulties arise in the church, or between brethren and sisters, it will be your duty to use your utmost endeavors to bring about a reconciliation, and restore unity and peace. Be faithful to the Lord, and he will endow thee with wisdom and understanding from on high, give you grace to do his work, and bless you in all your duties. The grace of God be with you. Amen."

The bishop then gives him the kiss of peace, and if any deacon is present, he does likewise, and wishes him God's grace and blessing.

The bishop then exhorts the church to receive the deacon in love, and to pray for him, that he may be blessed and strengthened in his calling; that through his efforts the church may be preserved in love and peace, and her rules and ordinances maintained to the glory of God, and the salvation of souls. The meeting is closed in the usual form.

CHOOSING AND ORDAINING A BISHOP, OR ELDER.*

When a bishop is to be chosen, the congregation calls a bishop from some neighboring congregation, who lays the matter before the members, and inquires into the character faithfulness, and abilities of their ministers; and if any are found possessing the necessary qualifications, according to the instructions of Paul, 2 Tim. 2:2; 3:2—8; and Tit. 1:6—9, the members are asked to give their voice for one among those who have already, for some time, been in the ministry, in the same manner as above stated in choosing a minister. Should all the

---

*The bishop or elder in the Mennonite church is simply the minister who has been ordained to the special charge of caring for, and officiating in the church of a certain prescribed district. This district may contain but one place of worship, or a number of places, which are at considerable distances from each other. He may have a number of fellow-ministers in his charge, to preach at the various places, and aid him in his work generally,

votes fall upon one person, the lot is not used, but when two or more are nominated, the matter is proceeded with in the same manner as in the choosing of a minister or deacon. In many places it is customary after the nominations are made, to defer the choosing and the ordination for some days, perhaps for a week or more; but frequently the nominating of candidates, the choosing by lot and ordination, all take place on the same day, as it may best suit the circumstances and convenience of the church.

On the day when the lot is to be cast, and the person chosen ordained, the officiating bishop reads 1 Tim. 3:1—9, and 1 Peter 5:1—4, or other appropriate Scriptures, and from these seek to set forth the solemn and important duties devolving upon a bishop, and the qualifications which he should possess.

After the bishop has been chosen, either by the united voice of the church or by lot the ordination takes place as follows: The newly elected bishop is requested to kneel, and the officiating bishop lays his hands upon his head (and if other bishops are present, they also at the same time lay their hands upon his head) and addresses him as follows:

"Dear Brother, you are chosen to the office of bishop in the church of Christ. It will be your duty to preach the word of God, to promulgate the pure doctrine of the Gospel of our salvation; to baptize and receive into the church those who believe, upon the confession of their faith, in the name of the Father, and of the Son, and of the Holy Ghost, and to teach them to observe all things whatsoever our Savior has commanded; and to administer the Communion of the Lord's Supper. It is also enjoined upon you to ex-communicate from the church, according to Matt. 18:17 and 1 Cor. 5, those who transgress the commands of Christ, and continue in their disobedience, and when they repent and return to obedience, to receive them again. It will also be your duty to officiate at the marriage of members of the church, to visit the sick and the afflicted, to comfort, encourage and strengthen them in their faith; indeed unto you we commit all the duties devolving upon a faithful steward in the house of the Lord, that in all things you may walk and do according to the Gospel. Therefore be not self-willed, not soon angry, but sober, just, holy, temperate, holding fast the faith as you have been taught, that you may be able by sound doctrine both to exhort and convince gainsayers. Be a faithful shepherd of the flock of God, that at last you may also be received by the Great Shepherd of souls with: 'Well done, good and faithful servant; enter thou into the joy of thy Lord.' May God, who has called you to this high and holy calling, anoint you with the Holy Ghost, give you grace and wisdom, and also bless you in all things, through His Son Jesus Christ, Amen."

The officiating bishop now takes the newly ordained bishop by the hand, raises him to his feet, gives him the brotherly salutation, and thus welcomes him as a co-laborer to the solemn duties to which he has been chosen.

He then addresses the members of the church as follows:

"Beloved brethren and sisters, Receive your bishop with joy; look upon him as chosen of God, and appointed over you to this important work. Pray for him, and manifest toward him the full measure of that great love which the Gospel requires. When he declares unto you the word of God, receive the truth, seek to obey, and submit yourselves unto him, for he watcheth over your souls as one who must give account, that he may do it with joy and not with grief. Heb. 13:17. Acknowledge him as one laboring among you, who is over you in the Lord, and admonishing you and teaching you the way of life everlasting; esteem him very highly for his work's sake, and be at peace among yourselves. 1 Thess. 5:12, 13. May God bless you and keep you as his own dear church, and finally bring you all to his eternal rest through Jesus Christ, our Lord, to whom be honor, and praise, and glory, forever. Amen."

A bishop then must be blameless, the husband of one wife, vigilant, sober, of good behavior [or modest], given to hospitality, apt to teach; not given to wine, no striker, not greedy of filthy lucre, but patient; not a brawler, not covetous; one that ruleth well his own house, having his children in subjection with all gravity; * * * not a novice, lest being lifted up with pride, he fall into the condemnation of the devil. Moreover he must have a good report of them which are without, lest he fall into reproach and the snare of the devil. 1 Tim. 3:2—4, 6, 7.

MARRIAGE FORMULA.

The marriage relation is the most important and sacred of any that can be formed in this life. It is of Divine origin, and was instituted of God for the happiness, preservation and welfare of mankind. It imposes upon us the most solemn obligations and duties, and from it spring the most momentous consequences. It is a union which surpasses even the natural ties of relationship. "For this cause shall a man leave his father and mother, and shall cleave to his wife, and they twain shall be one flesh."

Since the marriage relation then is one of such great importance, great care should be exercised in assuming it, and hence when two persons, who are members of the church, agree together to enter the married state, their names are published before the congregation, at the close of the public services, on at least two successive Sundays.*

---

*Since the system of Legal licenses has been established in most of the states, the custom of publishing in church is gradually becoming obsolete. In Canada and

After they have been twice published, and no cause has been presented against them, the marriage may at any time be solemnized.

The marriage ceremony, according to our present usage, generally takes place at the home of the bride. There is apparently no reason, however, why it should not be performed in the meeting-house, at the time of public services, according to the custom of our brethren in former times, and as is still the custom with some Mennonite churches.

The ceremony is conducted as follows: After the singing of a hymn, and a prayer appropriate to the occasion, the minister reads Mark 10:2—12. He then addresses the bridal pair, and explains the origin and institution of marriage, the duties and obligations it imposes, the sanctity of the relation into which they are placed by taking upon themselves the bonds of matrimony. He admonishes them to serve and fear God, lead a pious, virtuous life, love one another, be faithful, kind and affectionate, forbearing and patient, and to endure willingly the

---

some other places, they are required to be published three successive Sundays before the marriage ceremony is performed.

sorrows and trials which may be associated with their joys through life.

After the conclusion of the discourse, he addresses those present, saying:

Beloved friends: It has now been fully made known that A. B. and C. D. have agreed to enter into the bonds of matrimony, and no reason has been shown to prevent them. But if any one present should know of any just cause why these persons should not be joined in holy matrimony, let him now declare it.

If none is presented, the bishop or minister again addresses the bridegroom and bride as follows:

If it is still your desire to enter into the bonds of matrimony, you will arise.

Upon this they present themselves standing, before the minister, the bridegroom on the right of the bride. The minister then asks the following questions:

1. To both, Do you believe that matrimony is an ordinance instituted of God, and confirmed and sanctioned by Jesus Christ, and that you must therefore enter upon it in the fear of God?

Each *answers:* I do.

2. He then asks the bridegroom: Do you confess and declare that you are unmarried, and free from all other marriage relations and engagements whatsoever?

Answer: I am.

3. He then likewise asks the bride:

Do you confess and declare that you are unmarried, and free from all other marriage relations and engagements whatsoever?

Answer: I am.

4. To the bridegroom, A. B.:

Will you, in the presence of God, and these witnesses, take C. D., the sister by your side, to be your wedded wife; will you love and cherish her, provide and care for her in health and sickness, in prosperity and adversity, exercise patience, kindness and forbearance toward her, live with her in peace as becometh a faithful, christian husband; and, forsaking all others, keep yourself only unto her as long as you both shall live?

Answer: I will.

5. To the bride, C. D.:

Will you, in the presence of God and these witnesses, take A. B., the brother by your side, to be your wedded husband; will you love and cherish him in health and in sickness, in prosperity and in adversity, share with him the joys and sorrows of life, exercise patience, kindness and forbearance toward him as becometh a faithful christian wife; and, forsaking all others, keep yourself only unto him as long as you both shall live?

Answer: I will.

The minister then says:

You will now take each other by the right hand.

Upon which he takes their joined hands between his hands, or holds them in his right hand, and says:

The God of Abraham, the God of Isaac, and the God of Jacob be with you, and bless you abundantly, through Jesus Christ. Go forth as husband and wife, live in peace, fear God and keep his commandments. Amen.

The services are now closed with prayer, the singing of a hymn, and the benediction.

NOTE:—After the marriage ceremony is performed, and before the exercises are closed it is a custom with some, to read Eph 5: 15—33; Col. 3: 18, 19; 1 Tim. 2:8—14, and 1 Peter 3: 1—7, and give an exhortation concerning the duties which, as husband and wife, the newly married pair owe to each other. This, however, may very properly be left to the option of the officiating minister.

DEALING WITH TRANSGRESSORS.

When discord or difficulties occur between members of the church, the rule given in Matt. 18:15, 16, shall be strictly observed. If after a faithful effort the difficulties cannot be adjusted, and the parties do not become reconciled, the deacon shall use his whole influence to bring the contending parties to an understanding, and have them settle the matter between themselves. When this cannot be accomplished, the matter is laid before the church, so that, if possible, through the prayers and efforts of the whole brotherhood, the offending and erring ones may become enlightened and reconciled. If this cannot be done, a counsel is taken. If either of the parties are not willing to submit to this counsel of the church, and still continue in their disobedience and insubmission, they will be allowed some time for consideration, in which time the church should make further efforts to gain them; and if they do not then submit, acknowledge their errors, and ask forgiveness, they must be excluded from the church, according to Matt. 18:16.

When it appears that any member of the church walks disorderly, and does not observe the Gospel of Jesus Christ, and the rules and ordinances of the church, he shall be visited by the deacon, who shall faithfully endeavor to bring him to a sense of his duty, to show him the error of his ways, and thus bring him to confess the transgression, to repent of his sins, and ask forgiveness and the forbearance of the church. But if by repeated efforts this cannot be done, the matter must also be brought before the church, a counsel taken, and the transgressor dealt with in the same manner as above.*

When, however, a member of the church becomes a gross and flagrant transgressor before the world, as a drunkard, a thief, an adulterer, etc., no admonition is required. Such a corrupt and wicked person must at once, but upon positive evidence of such transgression, be excluded from the church, according to 1 Cor. 5, and 2 Cor. 13.

---

* Every accused member, however, before being expelled, should be visited and heard with regard to the accusation.

On these points Menno Simon says, "Behold, in this sense the Holy Scripture remains salutary unto us, and proceeds in its proper order, when, according to Matt. 18:15—18, one brother transgresses against another, three admonitions are given before excommunication; to a heretic, one or two (Tit. 3:10), and to an open offensive, sensual sinner, who is already condemned by the word, none at all." 1 Cor. 5; 2 Cor. 13.

Take heed to yourselves: If thy brother trespass against thee, rebuke him; and if he repent, forgive him: And if he trespass against thee seven times in a day, and seven times in a day turn again to thee, saying, I repent; thou shalt forgive him. Luke 17:3, 4.

Brethren, if a man be overtaken in a fault, ye which are spiritual, restore such a one in the spirit of meekness; considering thyself, lest thou also be tempted Bear ye one another's burdens and so fulfill the law of Christ. Gal. 6:1, 2.

Brethren, if any one of you do err from the truth, and one convert him, let him know, that he which converteth the sinner from the error of his way shall save a soul from death, and shall hide a multitude of sins. James 5:19, 20.

EXCOMMUNICATION.

When from any cause it becomes necessary to excommunicate a member of the church, the bishop, at the close of the usual public services, in the presence of the congregation reads Matt. 18: 15—18, or Tit. 3: 10, or 1 Cor. 5, according to the nature of the transgression of the person to be excomunicated, and then announces to them his name (and, if expedient and necessary, the transgression which he has committed), and declares him no longer a member of the church. He is, however, exhorted to repentance and amendment of life that he may be reclaimed to the favor of God and the fellowship of the church. The members are also instructed to do their duty in trying to win him by admonishing him as a brother (2 Thess. 3: 15) that the soul may be saved.

RECEIVING EXCOMMUNICATED PERSONS INTO THE CHURCH AGAIN.

When excommunicated persons see the error of their ways, sincerely repent of their sins, are willing to acknowledge and confess their transgressions, and ask forgiveness of those whom they have injured or offended, they shall again be received into the communion of the church. When the request to be restored is made by any such person, the matter is presented before the church, and a counsel is taken; and if the members are satisfied with his confession and evidences of repentance, he is received at the next, or a subsequent meeting.

In receiving him, the bishop asks:

1. Do you sincerely desire to be again received into the communion of the church of Christ?

2. Are you truly sorry for the sins which you have committed, and do you sincerely repent, and ask God and the church to forgive you; and do you promise by the grace and help

of God, and the aid of his Holy Spirit, henceforth to walk more circumspectly, and to submit yourself anew to Christ and his word, and faithfully to abide in the same until death?

If these questions are answered affirmatively, the bishop takes him by the hand and says:

Upon this confession which thou hast made before God and these witnesses, thou shalt again be acknowledged as a member of the body of Christ, and a brother (or sister) in the church; and so long as thou art faithful and abidest in the doctrine of his word, thou art his disciple indeed.

He then gives him the brotherly salutation, and says:

May God bless and strengthen thee and give thee grace to remain faithful unto the end, through Jesus Christ our Lord. Amen.

A RULE TO BE OBSERVED WHEN DIFFICULTIES OCCUR BETWEEN MEMBERS OF THE CHURCH.

When difficulties occur between members of the church, in relation to secular affairs, the deacon, in the first place, shall make an effort to bring them to terms, and settle the matter between themselves. When this cannot be accomplished, the deacon shall advise them to choose arbitrators from among the brethren in the church, whose duty it will be upon the appointed time, to examine the matter in dispute, receive the testimony of witnesses, and impartially, and to the best of their knowledge and judgment, decide the matter. They should especially endeavor so to decide, that both parties may be satisfied. Should it, however, be discovered that transgressions have been committed on either or on both sides, the arbitrators shall advise the deacon, who shall present the matter to the church. A counsel shall then be taken, and the case determined according to the nature and the circumstances therein involved.

But if one of the contending parties should be unwilling to submit to the decision of the arbitrators, and the counsel of the church, and continue in his self-righteousness and insubmission, a certain time for consideration of the matter should be given him, and if he then still refuses to submit and acknowledge his error, he must, according to Matt. 18:17, be excluded from the church, until he repents, becomes willing to acknowledge his error, and desires to be readmitted into the fellowship of the Church.

Funeral Services.

SCRIPTURE LESSONS APPROPRIATE FOR FUNERAL OCCASIONS.

1. The Burial of Sarah.—Gen. 23. Verses 10 to 17 may be omitted.
2. The Burial of Jacob.—Gen. 49:28—33; 50:1—13.
3. The Death of Absalom.—Gen. 18:31—33.
4. The Afflictions of Job.—Job 1.
5. Job's Extreme Anguish.—Job. 3:1—19.
6. Brevity and Uncertainty of Life.—Job 14.
7. The Frailty of Man.—Psa. 90.
8. Remembrance of God in Youth.—Eccl. 12:1—7.
9. Death of Lazarus.—John 11:1—27.
10. The Resurrection of Lazarus.—John 11:32—45.
11. The Resurrection of the Dead.—1 Cor. 15:12—58.
12. The happy State of the Righteous Dead.—2 Cor. 5:1—4; 1 Thess. 4:13—18.

The following lessons are also appropriate to be read when visiting believers who are sick. To these might be added *2 Kings 20:1—11; Isaiah 43:1—7; 44:1—8.*

13. The Blessedness of Affliction.–Heb. 12:1-11.
14. The Glory of those who are Victorious in Tribulations.—Rev. 7:9—17.
15. The Glory of the Heavenly City.—Rev. 21.
16. The Saints by the River of Life.—Rev. 22:1—5.

For all things *are* for your sakes, that the abundant grace might through the thanksgiving of many redound to the glory of God. For which cause we faint not; but though our outward man perish, yet the inward *man* is renewed day by day. For our light affliction, which is but for a moment, worketh for us a far more exceeding *and* eternal weight of glory; while we look not at the things which are seen, but at the things which are not seen: for the things which are seen *are* temporal; but the things which are not seen *are* eternal. 2 Cor. 4:15—18.

FUNERAL TEXTS.

For the Funeral of a Child.

Although affliction cometh not forth of the dust, neither doth trouble spring out of the ground: yet man is born unto trouble as the sparks fly upward. Job 5:6, 7.

Man *that is* born of a woman *is* of few days and full of trouble. He cometh forth like a flower, and is cut down; he fleeth also as a shadow, and continueth not. Job 14:1, 2.

I have said to corruption, *Thou art* my father: to the worm, *Thou art* my mother, and my sister. Job 17:14.

As *for* man, his days *are* as grass: as a flower of the field, so he flourisheth. For the wind passeth over it, and it is gone: and the place thereof shall know it no more. Psalm 103:15, 16.

A voice was heard in Ramah, lamentation, *and* bitter weeping: Rachel weeping for her children, refused to be comforted for her children, because they *were* not. Jer. 31:15.

And Jacob rent his clothes, and put sackcloth upon his loins, and mourned for his son many days. And all his sons and all his daughters rose up to comfort him; but he refused to be comforted; and he said, For I will go down into the grave unto my son mourning. Thus his father wept for him. Gen. 37:34, 35.

And Nathan departed unto his house. And the Lord struck the child that Uriah's wife bare unto David and it was very sick. David therefore besought God for the child: and David fasted, and went in, and lay all night upon the earth. And the elders of his house arose, *and went* to him, to raise him up from the earth: but he would not, neither did he eat bread with them. And it came to pass on the seventh day, that the child died. And the servants of David feared to tell him that the child was dead: for they said, Behold, while the child was yet alive, we spake unto him, and he would not hearken unto our voice: how will he then vex himself, if we tell him that the child is dead? But when David saw that his servants whispered, David perceived that the child was dead: therefore David said unto his servants, Is the child dead? And they said, He is dead. Then David arose from the earth, and washed, and anointed *himself*, and came into the house of the Lord, and worshiped: then he came to his own house; and when he required, they set bread before him, and he did eat. Then said his servants unto him, What thing *is* this that thou hast done? Thou didst fast and weep for the child, *while it was* alive; but when the child was dead, thou didst rise and eat bread. And he said, While the child was yet alive, I fasted and wept; for I said, Who can tell *whether* God will be gracious to me, that the child may live? But now he is dead, wherefore should I fast? Can I bring him back again? I shall go to him, but he shall not return to me. 2 Samuel 12:16—23.

And when the child was grown, it fell on a day, that he went out to his father to the reapers. And he said to his father, My head, my head! And he said to a lad, Carry him to his mother. And when he had taken him, and brought him to his mother. he sat on her knees till noon, and *then* died. And she went up and laid him on the bed of the man of God, and shut *the door* upon him, and went out. And she called to her husband, and said, Send me, I pray thee, one of the young men, and one of the asses, that I may run to the man of God, and come again. And he said, Wherefore wilt thou go to him to-day? *it is* neither new moon nor Sabbath. And she said, *It shall be* well. Then she saddled an ass, and said to her servant, Drive, and go forward; slack not *thy* riding for me, except I bid thee. So she went, and came unto the man of God to mount Carmel. And it came to pass, when the man of God saw her afar off, that he said to Gehazi his servant, Behold, *yonder is* the Shunammite: run now, I pray thee, to meet her, and say unto her, *Is it* well with thee? *is it* well with thy husband? *is it* well with the child? And she answered, It is well. 2 Kings 4:18—26.

I was dumb, I opened not my mouth; because thou didst it. Psalm 39:9.

The Lord gave, and the Lord hath taken away, blessed be the name of the Lord. Job. 1:21.

And they brought young children to him, that he should touch them; and *his* disciples rebuked those that brought *them*. But when Jesus saw *it*, he was much displeased, and said unto them, Suffer the little children to come unto me, and forbid them not; for of such is the kingdom of God. Verily, I say unto you, Whosoever shall not receive the kingdom of God as a little child, he shall not enter therein. And he took them up in his arms, put *his* hands upon them, and blessed them. Mark 10:13—16.

Take heed that ye despise not one of these little ones; for I say unto you, That in heaven their angels do always behold the face of my Father which is in heaven. Even so it is not the will of your Father which is in heaven, that one of these little ones should perish. Matt. 18:10—14.

NOTE. *These texts, or a part of them, read consecutively, may be used as a funeral lesson.*

FOR A YOUNG PERSON, OR A SUDDEN DEATH.

Man that is born of a woman is of few days, and full of trouble.

He cometh forth like a flower, and is cut down: He fleeth also as a shadow, and continueth not. Job 14:1, 2.

As for man, his days are as grass: as a flower of the field, so he flourisheth. For the wind passeth over it, and it is gone; and the place thereof shall know it no more. Psa. 103:15, 16.

Thou carriest them away as with a flood; they are as a sleep: in the morning they are like grass which groweth up. In the morning it flourisheth, and groweth up; in the evening it is cut down, and withereth. Psa. 90:5.

Behold, thou hast made my days as a handbreadth; and mine age is as nothing before thee: verily every man at his best state is altogether vanity. Psa. 39:5.

For we are strangers before thee, and sojourners, as were all our fathers: our days on the earth are as a shadow, and there is none abiding. 1 Chron. 29:15.

As the cloud is consumed and vanisheth away; so he that goeth down to the grave shall come up no more. He shall return no more to his house, neither shall his place know him any more. Job 7:9, 10.

Now my days are swifter than a post: they flee away, they see no good. They are passed away as the swift ships: as the eagle that hasteth to the prey. Job 9:25, 26.

My days are swifter than a weaver's shuttle, and are spent without hope. Job 7:6.

Boast not thyself of to-morrow; for thou knowest not what a day may bring forth. Prov. 27:1.

Go to now, ye that say, To-day or to-morrow we will go into such a city, and continue there a year, and buy and sell, and get gain. Whereas ye know not what shall be on the morrow. For what is your life? It is even a vapor, that appeareth for a little time, and then vanisheth away. James 4:13, 14.

See then that ye walk circumspectly, not as fools, but as wise, redeeming the time. because the days are evil. Eph. 5:15, 16.

For man knoweth not his time: as the fishes that are taken in an evil net; and as the birds that are caught in a snare; so are the sons of men snared in an evil time, when it falleth suddenly upon them. Eccl. 9:12.

There is but a step between me and death. 1. Samuel, 20:3.

Whatsoever thy hand findeth to do, do it with thy might; for there is no work, nor device, nor knowledge, nor wisdom, in the grave, whither thou goest. Eccl. 9:10.

Lord, make me to know mine end, and the measure of my days, what it is; that I may know how frail I am. Psa. 39:4.

So teach us to number our days, that we may apply our hearts unto wisdom. Psa. 90:12.

For a Middle-Aged Christian.

For what is your life? It is even a vapor, that appeareth for a little time, and then vanisheth away. James 4:14.

I have said to corruption, Thou art my father: to the worm, Thou art my mother, and my sister. Job 17:14.

But I would not have you to be ignorant, brethren, concerning them which are asleep, that ye sorrow not, even as others which have no hope. For if we believe that Jesus died and rose again, even so them also which sleep in Jesus will God bring with him. 1. Thess. 4:13, 14.

The wicked is driven away in his wickedness: but the righteous hath hope in his death. Prov. 14:32.

And he gave them their request; but sent leanness into their soul. Psa. 106:15.

For we know that, if our earthly house of this tabernacle were dissolved, we have a building of God, a house not made with hands, eternal in the heavens. 2. Cor. 5:1.

Therefore we are always confident, knowing that, whilst we are at home in the body, we are absent from the Lord. 2 Cor. 5:6.

And I heard a voice from heaven saying unto me, Write, Blessed are the dead which die in the Lord from henceforth: Yea saith the Spirit, that they may rest from their labors; and their works do follow them. Rev. 14:13.

And the ransomed of the Lord shall return, and come to Zion with songs and everlasting joy upon their heads: they shall obtain joy and gladness, and sorrow and sighing shall flee away. Isaiah 35:10.

And God shall wipe away all tears from their eyes; and there shall be no more death, neither sorrow, nor crying, neither shall there be any more pain: for the former things are passed away. Rev. 21:4.

These are they which came out of great tribulation, and have washed their robes, and made them white in the blood of the lamb. Therefore are they before the throne of God, and serve him day and night in his temple: and he that sitteth on the throne shall dwell among them. They shall hunger no more, neither thirst any more; neither shall the sun light on them, nor any heat. For the Lamb which is in the midst of the throne shall feed them, and shall lead them unto living fountains of waters: and God shall wipe away all tears from their eyes. Rev. 7:14—17.

For an Aged Christian.

For all our days are passed away in thy wrath: we spend our years as a tale that is told. The days of our years are threescore years and ten; and if by reason of strength they be fourscore years, yet is their strength labor and sorrow; for it is soon cut off, and we fly away. Psa. 90:9, 10.

As the cloud is consumed and vanisheth away; so he that goeth down to the grave shall come up no more. He shall return no more to his house, neither shall his place know him any more. Job 7:9, 10.

Your fathers, where are they? and the prophets, do they live forever? Zech. 1:5.

If a man die, shall he live again? All the days of my appointed time will I wait, till my change come. Thou shalt call, and I will answer thee: thou wilt have a desire to the work of thine hands. Job 14:14, 15.

For I know that my Redeemer liveth, and that he shall stand at the latter day upon the earth: And though after my skin worms destroy this body, yet in my flesh shall I see God: Whom I shall see for myself, and mine eyes shall behold, and not another; though my reins be consumed within me. Job 19:25—27.

For this corruptible must put on incorruption, and this mortal must put on immortality. 1 Cor. 15:53.

There is one glory of the sun, and another glory of the moon, and another glory of the stars; for one star differeth from another star in glory. So also is the resurrection of the dead. It is sown in corruption, it is raised in incorruption; it is sown in dishonor, it is raised in glory; it is sown in weakness, it is raised in power; it is sown a natural body, it is raised a spiritual body. There is a natural body, and there is a spiritual body. 1 Cor. 15:41—44.

Who shall change our vile body, that it may be fashioned like unto His glorious body, according to the working whereby he is able even to subdue all things unto himself. Phil. 3:21.

Blessed be the God and Father of our Lord Jesus Christ, which according to his abundant mercy hath begotten us again unto a lively hope by the resurrection of Jesus Christ from the dead, to an inheritance incorruptible, and undefiled, and that fadeth not away, reserved in heaven for you. 1 Peter 1:3, 4.

So when this corruptible shall have put on incorruption, and this mortal shall have put on immortality, then shall be brought to pass the saying that is written, Death is swallowed up in victory. O death, where is thy sting? O grave, where is thy victory? 1 Cor. 15:54, 55.

Then shall the righteous shine forth as the sun in the kingdom of their Father. Who hath ears to hear, let him hear. Matt. 13:43.

Let me die the death of the righteous, and let my last end be like his. Num. 23:10.

Also Ecclesiastes 12:1—7.

For an Aged Person.

There is no man that hath power over the spirit to retain the spirit; neither hath he power in the day of death; and there is no discharge in that war; neither shall wickedness deliver those that are given to it. Eccl. 8:8.

One dieth in his full strength, being wholly at ease and quiet. His breasts are full of milk, and his bones are moistened with marrow. And another dieth in the bitterness of his soul, and never eateth with pleasure. They shall lie down alike in the dust, and the worms shall cover them. Job 21:23—26.

What man is he that liveth, and shall not see death? shall he deliver his soul from the hand of the grave? Psa. 89:48.

They that trust in their wealth, and boast themselves in the multitude of their riches; none of them can by any means redeem his brother, nor give to God a ransom for him: that he should still live forever, and not see corruption. Psa. 49:6, 7, 9.

Is there not an appointed time to man upon earth? are not his days also like the days of a hireling? Job 7:1.

Seeing his days are determined, the number of his months are with thee, thou hast appointed his bounds that he cannot pass. Job 14:5.

Thou destroyest the hope of man. Thou prevailest forever against him, and he passeth; thou changest his countenance, and sendest him away. Job 14:19, 20.

For Various Occasions.

There is no man that hath power over the spirit to retain the spirit; neither hath he power in the day of death; and there is no discharge in that war; neither shall wickedness deliver those that are given to it. Eccl. 8:8.

For I know that thou wilt bring me to death, and to the house appointed for all living. Job 30:23.

And have hope toward God, which they themselves also allow, that there shall be a resurrection of the dead, both of the just and unjust. Acts 24:15.

For since by man came death, by man came also the resurrection of the dead. For as in Adam all die, even so in Christ shall all be made alive. 1 Cor. 15:21, 22.

Marvel not at this: for the hour is coming, in the which all that are in the graves shall hear his voice, and shall come forth; they that have done good, unto the resurrection of life; and they that have done evil, unto the resurrection of damnation. John 5:28, 29.

But some man will say, How are the dead raised up? and with what body do they come? 1 Cor. 15:35.

It is sown in corruption, it is raised in incorruption: it is sown in dishonor, it is raised in glory: it is sown in weakness, it is raised in power: it is sown a natural body, it is raised a spiritual body. There is a natural body, and there is a spiritual body. 1 Cor. 15:42—44.

For this corruptible must put on incorruption, and this mortal must put on immortality. 1 Cor. 15:53.

And as it is appointed unto men once to die, but after this the judgment. Heb. 9:27.

For we must all appear before the judgment seat of Christ; that everyone may receive the things done in his body, according to that he hath done, whether it be good or bad. 2 Cor. 5:10.

So then every one of us shall give account of himself to God. Rom. 14:12.

Because he hath appointed a day, in the which he will judge the world in righteousness by that man whom he hath ordained; whereof he hath given assurance unto all men, in that he hath raised him from the dead. Acts 17:31.

Be not deceived: God is not mocked: for whatsoever a man soweth, that shall he also reap. For he that soweth to his flesh shall of the flesh reap corruption; but he that soweth to the Spirit shall of the Spirit reap life everlasting. Gal. 6:7, 8.

When the Son of man shall come in his glory, and all the holy angels with him, then shall he sit upon the throne of his glory: and before him shall be gathered all nations: and he shall separate them one from another, as a shepherd divideth his sheep from the goats: and he shall set the sheep on his right hand, but the goats on the left. Then shall the King say unto them on his right hand, Come, ye blessed of my Father, inherit the kingdom prepared for you from the foundation of the world. Then shall he say also unto them on the left hand, Depart from me, ye cursed, into everlasting fire, prepared for the devil and his angels. And these shall go away into everlasting punishment: but the righteous into life eternal. Matt. 25:31—34; and 41, 46.

If the clouds be full of rain, they empty themselves upon the earth: and if the tree fall toward the south, or toward the north, in the place where the tree falleth, there it shall be. Eccl. 11:3.

And have hope toward God, which they themselves also allow, that there shall be a resurrection of the dead, both of the just and unjust. Acts 24:15.

He that is unjust, let him be unjust still: and he which is filthy, let him be filthy still: and he that is righteous, let him be righteous still: and he that is holy, let him be holy still. Rev. 22:11.

Jesus said unto her, I am the resurrection and the life: he that believeth in me, though he were dead, yet shall he live: And whosoever liveth and believeth in me shall never die. Believest thou this? John 11:25, 26.

For we brought nothing into this world, and it is certain we can carry nothing out. 1 Tim. 6:7.

For to me to live is Christ, and to die is gain. Phil. 1:21.

For which cause we faint not; but though our outward man perish, yet the inward man is renewed day by day. 2 Cor. 4:16.

But thanks be to God, which gives us the victory through our Lord Jesus Christ. 1 Cor. 15:57.

Now this I say, brethren, that flesh and blood cannot inherit the kingdom of God; neither doth corruption inherit incorruption. 1 Cor. 15:50.

And so it is written, The first man Adam was made a living soul; the last Adam was made a quickening spirit. Howbeit that was not first which is spiritual, but that which is natural; and afterward that which is spiritual. The first man is of the earth, earthy: the second man is of the Lord from heaven. 1 Cor. 15: 45—47.

For the wages of sin is death; but the gift of God is eternal life through Jesus Christ our Lord. Romans 6:23.

For I am now ready to be offered, and the time of my departure is at hand. I have fought a good fight, I have finished my course, I have kept the faith: Henceforth there is laid up for me a crown of righteousness, which the Lord, the righteous judge, shall give me at that day: and not to me only, but unto all them also that love his appearing. 2 Tim. 4:6—8.

SERVICES AT THE GRAVE.

The services may be closed immediately after the corpse is lowered into the grave, or the grave may be first filled. A hymn may be sung while the grave is being filled.

As a closing service the minister may say:

"Man that is born of a woman is of few days and full of trouble; he cometh forth like a flower and is cut down; he fleeth also as a shadow and continueth not." Job 14:1, 2. "For all flesh is as grass, and all the glory of man as the flower of grass. The grass withereth and the flower thereof falleth away; but the word of the Lord endureth forever." (1 Pet. 1:24, 25), in which word we have the promise of eternal life through our Lord Jesus Christ. Amen.

"I am the resurrection and the life," saith the Lord: "he that believeth in me, though he were dead, yet shall he live; and whosoever liveth and believeth in me shall never die." John 11:25, 26.

"I know *that* my Redeemer liveth and *that* he shall stand at the latter *day* upon the earth: and *though* after my skin *worms* destroy this *body*, yet in my flesh shall I see God." Job 19:25, 26.

"So when this corruptible shall have put on incorruption, and this mortal shall have put on immortality, then shall be brought to pass the saying that is written: Death is swallowed up in victory. Oh death, where is thy sting? O grave, where is thy victory?" 1 Cor. 15:54, 55.

"In my Father's house are many mansions: If it were not so, I would have told you. I go to prepare a place for you. And if I go and prepare a place for you, I will come again and receive you unto myself; that where I am, there ye may be also." John 14:2, 3.

"And God shall wipe away all tears from their eyes; and there shall be no more death, neither sorrow, nor crying, neither shall there be any more pain; for the former things are passed away." Rev. 21:4.

"Then shall the righteous shine forth as the sun in the Kingdom of their Father." Matt. 13:43.

"Wherefore comfort one another with these words." 1 Thess. 4:18.

"And I heard a voice from heaven saying unto me, Write, Blessed are the dead which die in the Lord from henceforth: Yea, saith the Spirit, that they may rest from their labors; and their works do follow them." Rev. 14:13.

The above passage (Rev. 14:13), may be used alone or from the closing sentence of any part of the foregoing passages, or any other appropriate remarks the minister may choose to select for the occasion.

Forasmuch as it has pleased Almighty God, in his wise providence, to take out of this world the soul of the departed,* we commit the body to the ground; earth to earth, ashes to ashes, dust to dust, and commit the soul to God who gave it, looking for the general resurrection in the last day and the life of the world to come through our Lord Jesus Christ; at whose second coming, in glorious majesty to judge the world, the earth and sea shall give up their dead; and

---

* Or of our deceased brother or sister as the case may be.

the corruptible bodies of those who sleep in him shall be changed, and made like unto his own glorious body; according to the mighty working whereby he is able to subdue all things unto himself.

The minister may then offer the following prayer, or any other one that is appropriate to the occasion.

Almighty God, with whom do live the spirits of those who depart hence in the Lord, and with whom the souls of the faithful, after they are delivered from the burden of the flesh, are in joy and felicity; we give thee hearty thanks for the good examples of all those thy servants, who, having finished their course in faith, do now rest from their labors. And we beseech thee, that we, with all those who are departed in the true faith of thy holy name, may have our perfect consummation and bliss, both in body and soul, in thy eternal and everlasting glory. O merciful Father, we humbly beseech thee to keep us from the death of sin, and enable us to walk in the life of righteousness, that when we depart this life, we may rest in Him who is the Resurrection and the life, and be found acceptable in thy sight, and receive that blessing which thy well-beloved Son shall then pronounce to all who love and fear thee, saying, Come, ye blessed of my Father, inherit the Kingdom prepared for you from the foundation of the world. Grant this, we beseech thee, through Jesus Christ, our Mediator and Redeemer. Amen.

The service may be closed by the benediction:

The grace of our Lord Jesus Christ, and the love of God our Father, and the fellowship of the Holy Spirit, be with us all evermore. *Amen.*

It will be observed that the services at the grave are given in sub-divisions as follows:

1. Scripture passages setting forth the frailty of human life.
2. Passages referring to the resurrection of the dead and the life beyond.
3. Passages directing the mind to the glory and blessedness of heaven.
4. A form committing the body to the earth, and directing the mind to Christ, who is Lord of all.
5. A prayer appropriate to such occasions.
6. The Benediction.

When the burial takes place before the sermon is preached in the church, which is the custom in many places, the benediction is not spoken at the grave, but at the close of service in the house. *When however the sermon is first preached and the burial takes place afterwards*, the services should always be closed with the benediction at the grave.

To repeat all this consecutively, forms an appropriate service at the grave and may, very properly, be used in this way, but in many cases it may be too long, and in some instances not altogether adapted to the circumstances. It will be well therefore for the minister to select from these such parts, as in his judgment, are most appropriate for the occasion. In some instances it is best to make the services very short, while in others a longer service may profitably be used. The minister should always use the utmost discretion in his selections.

The object of these lessons is not to establish an invariable form, but simply to suggest and direct to that which is proper, appropriate and edifying; and hence the services may be varied so as to best subserve the purpose for which they are designed.

APOSTOLIC CONFESSION OF FAITH.

I believe in God, the Father, Almighty Creator of heaven and earth: And in Jesus Christ, his only begotten Son our Lord; who was conceived by the Holy Ghost, born of the Virgin Mary, suffered under Pontius Pilate, was crucified, died, and was buried. He rose again from the dead. On the third day He ascended into heaven, where he sitteth on the right hand of God the Father Almighty, from whence he shall come to judge the living and the dead. I believe in the Holy Ghost; the General Christian Church; the Communion of Saints; the Forgiveness of sins; the Resurrection of the body, and the Life everlasting. Amen.

THE LORD'S PRAYER.

Our Father which art in heaven, hallowed be thy name. Thy kingdom come, Thy will be done on earth, as it is in heaven. Give us this day our daily bread. And forgive us our debts, as we forgive our debtors. And lead us not into temptation; but deliver us from evil: For thine is the kingdom, and the power, and the glory, for ever. Amen. Matt. 6:9—13.

PRAYER.

God be merciful to us, and bless us; and cause his face to shine upon us; that thy way may be known upon earth, thy saving health among all nations. Let the people praise thee. O God: let all the people praise thee. Oh let the nations be glad and sing for joy: for thou shalt judge the people righteously, and govern the nations upon the earth. Let the people praise thee, O God; let all the people praise thee. Then shall the earth yield her increase; and God, even our God, shall bless us. God shall bless us; and all the ends of the earth shall fear him. Psa. 67:1—7.

BENEDICTIONS.

The Grace of our Lord Jesus Christ, and the love of God, and the communion of the Holy Ghost, be with you all, Amen. 2 Cor. 13:14.

The Lord bless thee, and keep thee; the Lord make his face shine upon thee, and be gracious unto thee: the Lord lift up his countenance upon thee, and give thee peace. Numbers 6:24—26.

The grace of our Lord Jesus Christ be with you all. Amen. Rom. 16:24.

CONTENTS.

Administration of Baptism.................................... 53
Advent of Christ into the World, &c.................... 9
Choosing and Ordaining a Bishop or Elder 81
Choosing and Ordaining a Deacon........................ 79
Choosing and Ordaining a Minister...................... 74
Communion of the Lord's Supper........................ 68
Concerning God and the Creation of all things......... 5
Dealing With Transgressors................................ 91
Defense by Force... 25
Examination Preceding the Communion................. 64
Excommunication... 94
Excommunication, or Expulsion from the Church.... 27
Fall of Man... 7
Feet Washing.. 72
Funeral Lessons.. 99
Funeral Texts for a Child................................. 101
"   "   for an aged Christian........................ 110
"   "   for a middle aged Christian............... 108
"   "   for a young person, or a sudden Death 105
Holy Baptism.. 15
Marriage Formula.. 86
Matrimony... 23
Office of Civil Government................................ 24
Office of Teachers and Ministers,—male and female
    —in the Church... 17
Receiving Excommunicated Persons into the Church 95
Repentance and Amendment of Life..................... 14
Resurrection of the Dead, and the last Judgment..... 31
Rule to be observed when Difficulties occur............ 97
Shorter Catechism... 37
Shunning of those who are Expelled..................... 29
Swearing of Oaths... 26
The Church of Christ....................................... 16
The Law of Christ, which is the Holy Gospel, or the
    New Testament... 12
The Lord's Supper... 21
The Restoration of Man Through the Promise of the
    Coming of Christ....................................... 8
Washing of the Saints' feet................................ 22

www.ingramcontent.com/pod-product-compliance
Lightning Source LLC
Chambersburg PA
CBHW031343160426
43196CB00007B/721